Pelican Books
The Empty Hours

Maureen Oswin was born in Middlesex in 1931.
After leaving school she did a variety of different
jobs for seven years – teaching riding and working
in a hotel among them. Then she trained as a
teacher, and since 1960 she has worked with
handicapped children. She has a diploma in Social
Studies, and a diploma in the education of backward
and maladjusted children. In 1967 she was awarded
a travel bursary by the Spastics Society, to study
child care in institutions for handicapped children.

Maureen Oswin lives in Surrey, and teaches
handicapped children in a children's hospital. She
is also a member of various committees related to
Hospital Management and to the welfare of
handicapped children. She is the author of one
previous book, *Behaviour Problems amongst
Children with Cerebral Palsy*.

Maureen Oswin

The Empty Hours

A Study of the Week-end Life
of Handicapped Children
in Institutions

Penguin Books

Penguin Books Ltd, Harmondsworth,
Middlesex, England
Penguin Books Inc., 7110 Ambassador Road,
Baltimore, Maryland 21207, U.S.A.
Penguin Books Australia Ltd, Ringwood,
Victoria, Australia

First published by Allen Lane The Penguin Press 1971
Published in Pelican Books 1973

Copyright © Maureen Oswin, 1971, 1973

Made and printed in Great Britain by
Hazell Watson & Viney Ltd,
Aylesbury, Bucks
Set in Linotype Juliana

This book is sold subject to the condition that
it shall not, by way of trade or otherwise, be lent,
re-sold, hired out, or otherwise circulated without
the publisher's prior consent in any form of
binding or cover other than that in which it is
published and without a similar condition
including this condition being imposed on the
subsequent purchaser

Contents

Acknowledgements 7
Preface to the Pelican Edition 9

Part One   Handicaps and Hospitals
   Handicaps 15
   History 27
   Functions of Children's Hospitals Today 39
   The Development of Special Education 47
   The Development of Child-Care Services 49

Part Two   Children in Hospitals
   Introduction 53
1. Fieldway: a Residential School in the Country 55
2. Ridge Hospital 75
3. Larchdale: a Residential School in the Suburbs 96
4. 'Blue Ward': a Week-end for Children with Severe Mental Disabilities 119
   What does Hospitalization do to Children? 137

Part Three   People Who Work in Hospitals
   Teachers 153
   Assistants 169
   Nurses 173
   An Occupation–Play Therapist 182
   The Role of the Voluntary Worker in Long-Stay Children's Hospitals 185

Part Four   Questions and Answers
   Introduction 197
   The Problem 198
   A Child's Questions 225

Bibliography 227

Acknowledgements

The author gratefully acknowledges the generosity of the Spastics Society in helping to finance this study. Grateful thanks are also owed to: the staff in the Department of Health and Social Security Statistics Department and Library, who assisted with figures and books; the staff and children in the hospitals and schools which were visited; Sheila M. Tack and May Harding, and members of the Council for Children's Welfare, who gave a great deal of friendly encouragement over a number of years, and Professor Jack Tizard, of the University of London, whose interest and kind support made it possible to undertake this work.

Preface to the Pelican Edition
Progress? The Latest Developments

After hardback publication in 1971 I received many letters, from prospective volunteers wanting to help, from Voluntary Organizations letting me know what they already did to help long-stay hospital children, from ex-volunteers who had been 'put off' by unwelcoming staff, and from over-worked staff who wished that local authorities, hospital administrators and the Department of Health and Social Security would be more sympathetic to the problems in long-stay hospitals. Old-age pensioners have written, widows, and unhappy, sick, people who felt empathy with rejected children. Letters from elderly people have contained small gifts, money, old Christmas cards, and simple home-made toys. W.R.V.S. groups and Women's Institutes and Church organizations have made toys and clothes and sent them to hospital children. Due to sympathetic newspaper articles in the provincial and national press, e.g. the late Moira Keenan of *The Times*, the late Anne Allen of the *Sunday Mirror* and Brigid Keenan of the *Observer*, many long-stay hospital children have been made happier by receiving regular visits from voluntary 'aunties' and 'uncles'.

The National Association for the Welfare of Children in Hospital has worked tirelessly to improve long-stay hospital care, organizing conferences and meetings, as well as doing voluntary work in the wards. N.A.W.C.H. was set up initially to improve problems of short-term care and for many years worked to achieve improvements in this field, but has now turned its energy to reforming conditions in long-stay hospitals as well.

Sir Keith Joseph, the Secretary of State for the Social Services, has expressed grave personal concern about the problems of long-stay hospital children, and his compassionate interest has influenced D.H.S.S. policy, especially related to children who have lost touch with their families. In the Spring of 1972 a Government leaflet (H.M. 72.2) drew attention to the problems of children who were abandoned in hospital (*Children in Hospital: Maintenance of Family Links and Prevention of Abandonment*), and the Hospital Advisory Service appointed a paediatrician to its teams, who would look at particular problems related to handicapped children.

But any complacency we might feel when looking at the growing interest of the public or the Government can be quickly off-set when thinking of letters I have had from parents, expressing hopeless depression at what is *not* being done for their handicapped children, and their everlasting worry over what will happen to those children when they themselves get old and die. One sad letter asked for advice about a retarded son aged forty, for whom there was no prospect except a long-stay hospital. What hope could I offer except to repeat the empty cliché 'local authority provision should be improving over the next ten years or so'? But are there ever going to be enough local authority homes and hostels to cater for the needs of the many thousands of young and old mentally and/or physically handicapped people who need sheltered care and a home-life? It is currently popular to say 'abolish long-stay hospitals'. But is this realistic? I see little chance of local authority community care being available for *all* who need it. Many thousands of badly disabled people will *always* live in hospitals, and this reason, if no other, should give support to the argument that present hospitals should be upgraded as much as possible in order to provide good care *now* for those handicapped people already in hospital and for those who will never get out.

The problems remain. The children remain. For them, in the wards, there is little comfort to be got from thinking about vague future improvements. Young children live essentially in the present, and if that present is miserable, lonely, bare and boring, then it embraces their whole world. Going recently into a scrupulously clean hospital ward for long-stay handicapped children, I was shocked, saddened and then feebly, hopelessly angered; the children were all aged between four and eight; they were prettily dressed, beautifully clean, and in their cots, the cots being placed in a row down the centre of a shining, sunshine-filled, highly polished, well-painted bare ward. There the children sat, bright, intelligent, physically disabled, bored, lonely, no toys, no occupations, nothing to reach out to or to touch through the bars of their cots. Like battery hens, void lives in cot cages.

I was with a voluntary worker from N.A.W.C.H. and we asked the nurses for toys, only to be told that Sister always kept the toy cupboard locked up. Indeed, it *was* locked, with a chain on it as well, to make doubly sure that no one would get into it. So, we played with the children with imaginary toys. Invisible cups and saucers: pretend saucepans that we stood on their pillows, which served as pretend cookers: we had a dinner party: cradling the imaginary soup bowls in our hands, we drank invisible soup with noisy gusto, the children laughing as we sometimes spilt it down our fronts. They stirred our dinner vigorously as it cooked on their cookers, excited to see us pull faces at too much salt or because we had burnt our tongues. Finding some paper hankies in a surgical bowl we pretended that these were our wiping-up cloths, and we helped the children to carefully wash and wipe up the invisible dishes and put them away in imaginary dressers at the end of their cots. The ward became noisy, suddenly animated, full of brief laughter, the children flushed and happy at the fun they were getting. Then it was time to go. We looked back down the ward, polished and bare, not a toy in sight, not a sheet or pillow out of place. The battery children were quiet again now, and still. But, away at the end of the long room, Jessy sat, bright-eyed and bolt upright in her tidy cot, clutching a paper hankie, still busy at wiping up an invisible pan.

'Wait,' she called. 'Come back, come *back*, I've found this greasy pot under the cooker, will you hang it on my dresser for me?'

Maureen Oswin
September 1972

Part One
Handicaps and Hospitals

Handicaps

Few of us will be lucky enough to complete our lives without being handicapped. Although not readily acknowledging the hard reality of it, we are all aware that, as we grow older, most of us become less able in our minds and bodies. There are the slight handicaps of short sight, imperfect hearing or the odd twinge of rheumatism, which we casually accept; there are the chronic handicaps of migraine, arthritis, bronchitis, which are faced with courage by countless sufferers and endlessly investigated by researchers. And there is the more dramatic onset of those serious handicaps which shock us when we meet them in our once fit friends or relatives, and which crudely remind us that our lives are quite short and vulnerable.

We may visit a friend who has had a 'stroke'; our embarrassment and pity at her sudden physical predicament is intensified by her valiant efforts to control dribbles and slurred speech and her childlike pride in her first teetering steps clutching some physiotherapy contraption. Mixed with our pity may be a creeping fear: our friend has entered a world unknown to most of us, become a member of that group we call 'handicapped'; we are afraid because the world of the handicapped suddenly appears very easy to enter.

When that adult friend becomes handicapped we are naturally shocked, frightened, perhaps even angry. What did he or she do to deserve it? Not wanting to believe that illness and handicap can strike anyone as an inevitable part of our living and dying, we look for reasons: he must have been living too well, drinking too much, eating the wrong food, smoking – by finding reasons we may successfully reassure ourselves that it cannot, will not, happen to us because we do not live too well, drink too much, eat the wrong food or smoke. A person chooses his own life, we argue; if he does things that shorten it, or worsen it, then the choice was his.

But many people are handicapped all their lives, born like it. Children are handicapped. How do we try and account for the handicaps of children? Some people actually say: 'Well, we might have guessed Mrs S. would have had that mongol baby, she always seemed a bit funny.' Or, 'Of course, it is not surprising when you think of Mrs T.'s spastic child. Her mother being all crippled up and Mr T. going off like that and leaving her.'

We group ourselves: there is the in-group of the fit families, and the out-group of families who have sundry misfortunes and whose children are handicapped. We always want to find some way to account for the deviation; perhaps by doing this we hope to protect ourselves against the likelihood of having a handicapped child of our own, so we try and find defects in the parents' lives. We are reluctant to believe that such cruel misfortune can occur to the most ordinary, happy and healthy families. But it can and does. There are thought to be approximately a quarter of a million children in this country today who have some form of handicap.

How much do we really understand about handicaps in childhood? Many people are unaware of the *variety* of children's handicaps. This ignorance may be due to non-involvement; it is easy to group all the handicaps together, call the victims 'spastics' or 'mongols' and not look too closely. But, by doing this, we reinforce our in-group attitude and fail to perceive the variety of handicaps and the individuality of those who are affected. The in-group attitude is never so evident as when we see several people all together, with embarrassing, distressing and obviously incurable handicaps.

Taking a group of handicapped children to a Zoo one day I was made brutally aware of the passive strength of the in-group. We had a group of children from a hospital, some spastic, some emotionally maladjusted, some with spinal diseases. We gathered our children's wheel-chairs to look at the lions and tigers. Two large junior-school groups came along, also to look at the lions and tigers. But the far greater attraction for the ordinary school children was our group of handicapped children.

'Look at them,' the whispers went round. Some of the school

children turned their backs on the lions and watched our wheelchair children uninhibitedly. The teachers looked pitying and embarrassed and they glanced away; but the children were interested and curious. At what stage in life do we progress from the honest curiosity of the young to that passive, strong adult pity which half-understands, knows fear and sterile embarrassment as its main emotion and chooses non-involvement as its main defence?

Junior-age children are open-minded and eager to learn. Should they share their schools with handicapped children, so they all become familiar with each other at an early age?

The tendency to group all the varieties of children's handicaps together, the lack of basic knowledge, causes distress to families and results in misunderstandings. The mother of a very slightly handicapped child said: 'The teachers at the infant school didn't understand that Jenny was bright, they thought because she was spastic that she was silly, and they always called her "that dear mongol child" and treated her like a baby.'

The mother of a mongol boy was distressed because neighbours believed her child was a 'psychopath' and would molest the younger children in the road. The parents of children injured by the thalidomide drug have sometimes had to convince friends and neighbours that their children were not necessarily mentally backward because they were minus their limbs.

The most common mistake made about handicapped children is the belief that a physical handicap includes a mental handicap as well. But this is not true, for a grossly physically deformed child, confined to a wheel-chair and needing someone to feed and wash him and see to his personal care, may still have a brain as alert and perceptive as an agile sportsman.

Another mistake is to assume that all physically handicapped children possess *above average* intelligence. This assumption may have been encouraged by the early publicity efforts of some Voluntary Societies who wanted to convince the public that physically handicapped children are not always mentally dull.

One of the dangers of making assumptions about handicapped children is that we may create pressures for them. For example, if we believe that all spastic children are intelligent then we may make intellectual demands that a dull or average spastic child will be quite unable to satisfy. Or, by assuming that all mongol children are extremely contented, we may see little wrong in shutting them into institutions which lack stimulations. We blithely think they will be happy anywhere.

Each handicapped child is an individual person. The population of children with handicaps possesses as wide a range of intellectual abilities and personality differences as will be found in the general population of people without handicaps. Children with handicaps should only be classed as a special group if such grouping will administratively benefit them, for example, when considering the sort of treatment they require, or the design of physical aids, design of buildings, or the training of staff.

What different handicaps are there amongst children?

First, there are the physical handicaps. The largest group of physically handicapped children are those we call 'spastic'; the word 'spastic' is a lay term, the correct description being cerebral palsy, which broadly describes a variety of conditions which may affect a child when his immature brain has suffered irreversible damage. Cerebral palsy will affect the child's movements and bodily functions and sometimes (but not always) his mental ability as well. The cerebral damage will have occurred very early in the child's life, perhaps being caused by birth damage, or some high-fever illness, or pre-birth incident; multiple births carry a risk of cerebral palsy.

The child with cerebral palsy may:

(a) Be so slightly handicapped that it is barely discernible, beyond perhaps a tendency to clumsiness, lack of physical dexterity, an inability to concentrate and a slight limp of one leg, or loss of the use of one arm.

(b) He may have a fairly serious disability involving loss of movement down one side, or below the waist, or permanent writhing movements, and/or deafness, speech disorders, and/or mental impairment.

(c) Be totally handicapped, speechless and perhaps with a mental disability as well; he will have to rely on other people to wash him, dress him, feed him and toilet him, all the days of his long life.

Handicaps and Hospitals 19

The intelligence of children with cerebral palsy can vary from serious mental subnormality up to above average. The most physically handicapped cerebral palsied children are not necessarily the most mentally handicapped; some of those who are totally physically handicapped may be intelligent, although quite unable to care for themselves physically. The tragedy of being cerebral palsied is that these children sometimes look very peculiar. They may writhe and wriggle, or dribble or speak with loud slurring voices, they may find emotional and physical control very difficult, especially when exciting and interesting things are happening. The life expectancy of children with cerebral palsy is average.

In 1968 there were 2,765 children with cerebral palsy in Special Schools for Physically Handicapped and Delicate Children. Many others would be in hospitals for the physically ill, or hospitals for the subnormal, or in training centres, or at home; some of those with only a slight handicap would be in ordinary schools.

Another condition which accounts for a number of handicapped children is spina bifida, which is a defect caused by some of the bones of the spine failing to develop properly; in simple terms, the spine has a division in it. Some children with spina bifida are very handicapped, but, as in cerebral palsy, there are degrees of handicap varying from the barely discernible to severe paralysis of the lower limbs and loss of bladder control and/or some mental impairment. Sometimes the child may have hydrocephalus, caused by the spinal defect interfering with the correct flow of spinal fluid to the skull and making the skull enlarge. Hydrocephalus can cause brain damage and additional physical and mental handicaps, so the children need an early operation to insert a control valve at the base of the skull which will prevent a build-up of fluid in the skull

When babies are born with spina bifida they can be helped by having an operation to correct their spine defect; the earlier the operation is performed the greater is the chance of success, so many babies are operated on when only a few hours or a day old. Because paralysis of the lower limbs sometimes causes incontinence, which is a serious social stigma, there may have to be another operation for girls with spina bifida to fit them with a urine drainage bag; this gives them independence socially. They usually have this operation when they reach infant or junior-school age.

Another complication associated with loss of sensation in the lower limbs is that there may be danger of the children getting a sore or a burn, bruised badly or even a bone fracture, without at first being aware of it. Because of this the children need to be trained to look after themselves sensibly, e.g. to inspect their lower body for sores developing, not to sit on hot pipes or have hot water bottles too hot, and to seek early attention for cuts and bruises round their legs.

At one time, very few spina bifida babies survived for long, but the early operation is now becoming so successful that there is an increasing number of children handicapped by spina bifida in Special Schools. In January 1968 there were 1,046 children with spina bifida handicaps in Special Schools for Physically Handicapped and Delicate Children. The intelligence of these children varies from above average to subnormality. In *The Health of the School Child*, reference is made to a study of 100 babies treated in Sheffield Children's Hospital by the early spine operation. In a follow-up study of these babies over a period of five years (1959–64) seventy survived the operation, fifty-five of them developed normal intelligence, ten were educationally subnormal, and five were too mentally subnormal to be able to benefit from a school education.

The Registrar-General's estimate of the incidence of spina bifida is 1·73 for every 1,000 live births. Some of these children need a considerable amount of physical care because they have a tendency to illnesses caused by chest, kidney or bladder infections.

Another sort of physical handicap is that of limb deficiency. Children minus one or more limbs need not suffer from brain damage or mental subnormality, and they possess the normal range of intellectual abilities found in any cross-section of the population. There have been instances of great courage shown by people with limb deficiencies, e.g. it is not unknown for women minus arms to marry and bring up a family, managing to cook and clean and even to change nappies with their feet. Modern inventions may help these children by providing artificial aids, but if

Handicaps and Hospitals 21

they do not have any residual limb then the devices may be very difficult to fit.

Children who were damaged by thalidomide sometimes have a small 'flapper', or remnant of a finger, foot or hand on the stump of their shoulder or thigh. They may learn to make use of this tiny limb to hold a pencil or a cup or spoon and fork; they can also make use of it for the fitting and manipulation of a mechanical (often powered) aid. Sometimes the thalidomide caused additional damage to the babies' eye and ear formation so that they were born blind and/or deaf.

Muscular dystrophy is another type of physical handicap. This generally affects boys, being a rare (but not completely unknown) disease in girls. The boy with muscular dystrophy gets progressively weaker as he gets older, until he is finally confined to a wheel-chair with his body perhaps supported by a jacket. In early childhood he would have been a normal running, active little boy, but his condition would have started showing between four and six and from then on he would slowly weaken. The tragedy of muscular dystrophy is that it 'runs in families', being transmitted from the mother to her sons. Three or four brothers in one family may be affected, and when the sister of the boys gets married she can pass it on to her own sons.

The mothers and sisters of boys with muscular dystrophy have sometimes consented to sterilization in order to prevent passing it on to any more boys. The life expectancy of these boys is not much more than eighteen to twenty-one years, but some have been known to live on into their thirties or forties; they run a high risk of pneumonia and other chest infections. As a group, their intellectual ability will cover as wide a range as any cross-section of the population.

Other physical handicaps and physical weaknesses in childhood can be caused by poliomyelitis, tuberculosis, haemophilia, rheumatism, heart diseases and varied orthopaedic disorders such as congenital hip dislocation, 'brittle bones' and spinal diseases or deformities.

Acute poliomyelitis has been largely eradicated in this country since the success of vaccination against it. But there are still numbers of young adults and adolescents who were left physically handicapped by the earlier epidemics, and who now live permanently in Homes for the disabled, or in long-stay hospitals. Some young adults have to rely on respirator machines in order to breath, others are confined to wheel-chairs, or get about with the aid of calipers or sticks. In 1968 there were 442 post-poliomyelitis handicapped children in Special Schools for Physically Handicapped and Delicate Children. Some of these children had caught the disease when abroad.

Haemophilia is a hereditary blood disease affecting the coagulation of the blood and resulting in a tendency to bleed excessively. Only boys are affected. Sometimes an ordinary ball game, or even a bumpy car ride, can set up internal bleeding into the child's joints; there is some risk that the joint haemorrhages may cause permanent disability if not attended to. The boy with haemophilia may have to lead a gentler life than most boys and have to attend a Special School for delicate children and be hospitalized for intermittent periods during his life. In 1968 there were 177 boys with haemophilia in Special Schools for Physically Handicapped and Delicate Children.

Some young people spend their childhood and adolescence in and out of hospitals because of recurrent bouts of rheumatism. One of the main problems for these children is that their education may be constantly interrupted by periods in hospitals or resting at home. In 1966 there were 1,500 children under fifteen in hospitals because of rheumatic fever.

Heart diseases can be related to rheumatic conditions or to congenital disorders. Heart surgery helps many children with congenital heart disorders, but there are still numbers of them who have to lead rather quiet lives in Special Schools or hospitals until they are ready for their operations. In 1968 there were 708 children with congenital and rheumatic heart diseases in Special Schools for Physically Handicapped and Delicate Children.

Asthma is another disease which may keep a child in a Special School, or in hospital for periods. When there are also home or family troubles as a contributory cause the child may go to a Residential Special School. It is estimated that approximately 150,000 children may have asthma for some period during their life at school; perhaps it might be only a short, temporary bout of the illness, but for some it might mean recurrent long spells which may keep the child in the medical wards of children's hospitals for several months. Asthma is the most common reason for being admitted to a Special School for Delicate Children.

Today there is an increasing number of children who have been injured in road accidents and left permanently disabled by limb, head, spine or internal injuries. They may be confined to wheelchairs, or get about with the aid of calipers and sticks. Sometimes they manage to return to ordinary schools despite being disabled, but often they have to go to Special Schools; some of them remain in hospitals permanently. There are some road-accident children who have survived terrible head-injuries which fifteen or twenty years ago would have killed them quickly, but today they are saved by modern technological skill and medical care. They are, however, irreversibly brain-damaged: they may remain deeply unconscious for weeks or months and then reawaken to a strange new life of handicaps, perhaps having a loss of movement in one or more limbs, a speech defect, a change in personality and intellect, or even a serious mental impairment. These children, after having once been ordinary, running, jumping, lively children, have now become 'spastics', and sadly enough it is generally through no fault of their own. They are truly the twilight children of the twentieth century, being not only the victims of the increased traffic brought about by present-day affluence but, paradoxically, the victims also of the compassion and modern skill of the doctors and nurses in special-care units who helped them to live against all conceivable odds.

Mentally Handicapped Children

Mental handicap is an 'umbrella term' covering a wide variety of illnesses and disease, and a wide variation in mental ability. Some mentally handicapped children will also be physically handicapped with cerebral palsy or spina bifida; some may have the additional problems of deafness, blindness and epilepsy.

A common misconception is that all mentally subnormal children belong to a vast sub-group of people who all have *equal* mental disabilities. But this is not so; for example, in a room containing a small group of mentally subnormal children there might be a child with cerebral palsy and a child with spina bifida sitting in wheel-chairs, there might be a mongol child, and two children classed as seriously subnormal. All five of these children will come under the umbrella term of mentally handicapped, all will be mentally less able in relation to the average person, but, if we watched that group of five children we would notice wide variations in the abilities of each individual child. The cerebral palsied child may be able to read a simple story to the seriously subnormal children, the child with spina bifida might help the child with mongolism to do a puzzle, later on one of the seriously subnormal children might fetch them a plate of biscuits and share it round for their mid-morning break. Helped by a knowledgeable adult they can live in harmony, each making use of the abilities they have, in order to help one another. Their intellectual ability will be below the standard demanded of most people in the world today, but they do represent a miniature society in their own right for they have a *varied range* of physical and mental abilities and they share their resources and divide their jobs according to their abilities. It is a gross error to imagine that all children with mental handicaps are of equally poor ability, for there are wide degrees of mental handicap in the same way as there are degrees of physical handicap.

Some mentally handicapped children go to Schools for Educationally Sub-Normal Children (ESN Schools). In 1968 there were 60,207 children who were already receiving some form of special education for ESN children or were waiting for a place.

Prior to 1971 some mentally retarded children were thought too subnormal to benefit from education under the DES. These children came under the Local Authority health departments for their education and they attended Local Authority day training centres; or, if there was not a training centre, they stayed at home all day. And the thousands of very subnormal children living in hospitals had a limited form of training-centre education within their hospital, organized by the hospital authorities.

In 1971 the Education (Handicapped Children) Act placed all subnormal children, whether living in hospitals or at home, under the administrative control of the DES, in the same way as all other handicapped children. In 1965 there were 18,770 Local Authority training centre places for subnormal children, and it is planned for these to be increased to 27,061 places in 1971. In 1970 there were 11,809 young people under twenty in subnormality hospitals, and 6,627 of these were aged under fourteen.

Some mentally handicapped children are not mentally backward, and might even be above average intelligence, but they have a temporary or permanent emotional or personality disorder which prevents them from behaving in a way normally accepted by society. These children are considered to be mentally ill rather than mentally subnormal. They are often desperately unhappy and cut off from enjoying ordinary family and community life, and in some cases their illness may cause them to function like a mentally subnormal child or give rise to physical illnesses.

There are degrees of severity in mental illness. Some children will only have a slight temporary illness and can be helped by attending a Child Guidance Clinic, others may go to a Special School for Maladjusted Children, but there are some more seriously ill children who may have long-term in-patient care in hospitals for the mentally ill.

In 1968 the figures for children in Special Schools for Maladjusted Children, or on the waiting list for a place, were 11,417; these included children receiving education at home or in special units. The Ministry of Health figures for children in hospitals for the mentally ill in 1970 were 1,732 aged under twenty, of whom 540 were aged under fourteen.

'Autistic' children, and children with schizophrenia, are usually considered to come into the category of mentally ill children. They may be placed in hospitals for the mentally ill, or in Local Authority training centres, or in Local Authority Special Schools, or in Special School Units attached to hospitals, or they may go to hospitals for the subnormal. Because the handicap of childhood autism is so complicated and has various forms and is not fully understood yet, these children may not receive the most suitable educational placement and help that they really need.

*

The life expectancy of handicapped children is sometimes believed to be less than average, but apart from particular illnesses, such as muscular dystrophy, this is not true. Because of general overall frailty some totally physically handicapped children run a high risk of chest infections, but the present-day standard of living and use of antibiotic drugs enables most handicapped children to have a normal life span.

A hundred years ago, however, many children with the handicaps discussed here would not have survived beyond childhood and some no longer than a few days or weeks. Those who did survive might have been hidden at home, some lucky ones may have received training from a Charity or Church organization, others may have gone to Poor Law Workhouse infirmaries or large asylums.

Life for everyone in the last century was a great deal harder than it is today. Just a brief look round an old country cemetery shows how common it was for children to die very young; tuberculosis was widespread, there were recurrent epidemics of fevers, and with the low standards of living and poor obstetrics, it was not uncommon for seven or eight children of one family to die before they reached the age of ten. It was truly the 'survival of the fittest' in the last century, and even those 'fittest' would have been poor specimens beside the healthy children of today. Efforts are made today to help even the most unfit children to survive, because we have the medical and technical skills to help them through their tremulous baby days.

How do we care for these children who are going to need our help for longer than other children because they are handicapped? Is our system planned and organized to match twentieth-century living standards and knowledge, or is it a patchy standard of care which has slowly evolved from a hotch-potch of nineteenth-century traditions and charities and half-rectified mistakes, and new half-understood theories? In order to try and understand a little about the care of handicapped children in hospital today it is necessary first to look briefly at the development of hospitals.

History

The history of caring for the handicapped and the sick since 1800 is intrinsically linked with the way the state cared for the destitute, the unemployed and the work-shy, and how private enterprise cared for the acutely ill. At the same time as state concern for the poor, the unemployed, the homeless, the aged and sick was leading to the founding of the big Poor Law Workhouses and asylums, there was also a growth of hospitals which were used by the acutely ill of the more fortunate classes; in addition, various charity organizations were developed to give help to some particular group which took their interest, e.g. the blind, the 'deserving poor', 'cripples' or the deaf.

So, on the one hand, there was a rapid growth of voluntary hospitals (which today we would call private hospitals) which took care of the acutely ill who were in a secure financial position or who had an employer who would finance their medical treatment; and, on the other hand, there were the big Poor Law Workhouses whose main function was to accommodate the unemployed and the destitute but which also took in a high percentage of homeless people who were chronically handicapped, aged and senile, mentally subnormal, mentally ill and physically ill.

The founding of the voluntary hospitals in the eighteenth and nineteenth centuries was aided by the philanthropic desire of rich people to help the ill, for it was a mark of status to take part in founding a voluntary hospital. These hospitals mostly treated people with acute but curable illnesses, such as 'stones', operable cancers, amputations, some fevers, accidents and anything else that might manage to get cured, or at least appear to be responding to treatment before the patient finally died.

In the eighteenth century there were very few hospitals in England and Wales, (there were only seven in London in 1780), while in 1800 there was only one bed to 5,000 people in the whole of England and Wales; a great contrast to 1961, when there was one bed to 175 people, serving a far larger population. In the first half of the nineteenth century there was an increase of hospital patients from 3,000 to 8,000 in England and Wales.

The big increase in numbers of hospital patients did not indicate a rapid rise in diseases (although there were plenty of epidemics) but it showed a steady growth in hospitals. Hospitals then were highly prone to infections and the patients stood a risk of picking up illnesses from each other. It is astonishing to think of the many seriously ill people who must at one time have been nursed entirely at home by their own families, perhaps having their illness complicated by ignorance; but at least they did not risk picking up an additional disease from a germ-ridden hospital ward. Home nursing books were in frequent use in many families and some of the books contained good homely advice, e.g. they recommended that the best way to deal with bugs that might be crawling up on to the beds and harming the patient was to stand the legs of the bed in little pans of water.

In the eighteenth century and the first part of the nineteenth century sick children were not often admitted to hospitals, and there were no hospitals specially for children, or children's wards. This was partly because young children were so prone to carrying infections that it was thought unwise to risk admitting them in case they started some epidemic in the wards; and it was partly due to the feeling that it was unwise to separate a young child from his mother in case he fretted. If a child *did* have to go into hospital it was thought best for the mother to go with him. But most sick children were nursed at home because a hospital full of nurses and mothers clashing in their opinions about the child inevitably led to difficulties.

Florence Nightingale believed that it was better not to segregate sick children in special children's wards or children's hospitals, and she recommended that babies and girls should be put into the women's wards and the older boys into men's wards so that the adult patients might take part in caring for them. However, this idea did not develop. In 1851 the first children's hospital was opened, in Liverpool. In 1852 Great Ormond Street Hospital was opened, the first hospital for children in London. By the 1860s there were six hospitals for children in London and six in the provinces. These hospitals generally took children between the ages of two and twelve. It was not thought right to separate a child under two from his family, but in urgent circumstances a child under two could be admitted, with or without his mother.

Handicaps and Hospitals 29

All the voluntary hospitals which were opening were financed partly from charitable funds and endowments and partly by small payments made by the patients or their families. Some employers would pay for their employees' medical treatment as an in-patient, and sometimes a benefactor of a hospital would give a letter nominating an employee, or a friend, or some poor person in whom he had an interest, to receive treatment. To have this 'subscriber's letter' was a coveted ticket to hospital. The voluntary hospitals mainly accepted short-stay curable cases, and they were becoming more and more selective during this period of nineteenth-century hospital development; they were in a position to pick and choose their patients, according to the patient's curability, or medical interest, or financial position and connections. Chronically ill or handicapped people were usually cared for at home.

But what was happening to poor people who were ill, did not know anyone connected with hospitals and whose illness was not particularly interesting to the doctors? And what was happening to the chronically handicapped who were destitute? These people usually had to go to the Poor Law Workhouses. There were about 50,000 sick people in Workhouses in 1861. These sick people were of the type that the voluntary hospitals could not, or would not, accept; they consisted of adults and children with skin diseases, epilepsy, tuberculosis, venereal diseases, the chronically sick, the mentally ill and mentally subnormal, the senile and the aged – all being without any financial security.

Poor Law Workhouses were intended to be uncomfortable places providing temporary accommodation of a harsh and punitive nature, which would deter work-shy or malingering persons who might have had ideas about living off public funds. The philosophy behind the Poor Law Workhouse was that an uncomfortable spell inside one would soon send the lazy physically fit person out looking for honest work again. These buildings were totally unsuitable for the many sick, handicapped and aged who were forced to live in them solely because they had no financial means of buying care for themselves. The domestic work of the Workhouse was often done by unpaid pauper inmates, so sick or handicapped children would be cared for by untrained and dirty paupers in conditions which did little to help their handicaps and probably made them much worse.

The physical conditions of the Workhouses in the mid nineteenth century were often disgusting and grossly overcrowded. One London Workhouse is recorded as having forty young girls sharing thirteen beds. Combs and brushes were scarce, and bathroom and toilet facilities completely inadequate; it was not unknown for sick and handicapped inmates to have to share one towel with thirty others, and to have to use chamber-pots to wash in. The smells inside these places must have been indescribable. There were few occupations or amusements for the inmates and many had to spend miserable years just lying and looking at each other or the bare walls.

The staffing of the sick departments of the Workhouses was very poor; the unpaid and untrained 'pauper nurses' who helped to look after the handicapped and sick were themselves destitute inmates. Sometimes they were supervised by a paid 'nurse', but she might not have had any real hospital experience, perhaps being merely a laundress. Many of the 'nurses' were drunkards.

The jobs of Workhouse Medical Officer and District Medical Officer were often combined. It was a badly paid job: sometimes the salary was as low as £100 to £200 per year. Although the Medical Officer to a Workhouse was a qualified doctor, the status of the job was considered to be far inferior to that of the actual Master of the Workhouse. As the powerful Masters of Workhouses were often only ex-Army men with no special training in dealing with sick or destitute people and with no knowledge of hygiene, it is easy to imagine that many arguments must have developed between the more educated and socially superior Medical Officers and the often uncouth Masters. The Masters' ideas on how to run the Workhouses were based on punitive measures aimed at deterring public scroungers and not on caring for the sick, the handicapped and the aged.

So, into these vast prison-like buildings, into an atmosphere of staff tensions, poor environmental conditions, sickness and distress, hundreds of helpless sick people were herded, their only 'crime' being that they were poor, unemployed and homeless. They varied in age from mere infants to the very aged and senile; they had no hope of cure for their ills and no financial security to give them a means of ever getting out again. They were at the mercy of the staff, subject to cruel whims, suffering from ignorant handling, and having additional ills heaped on to them because of poor diet, overcrowding, insufficient ventilation and warmth, and the psychological strain of boredom, semi-imprisonment and each other's proximity.

A whole family could be put into a Workhouse if they were destitute through father having been long-unemployed due to illness, an accident or a poor season's harvest. Once inside, the men would be separated from the women and children; even aged grandparents would be separated from each other. If the family contained a handicapped or sick child he would be separated from the rest of his family and be placed amongst a variety of old and young infirm people suffering from mental illness, mental subnormality, senility, chronic handicaps and numerous physical illnesses with distressing symptoms.

A cerebral palsied child in those days could spend years confined to a bug-infested bed, staring at a bare wall, treated as a drooling imbecile by ignorant drunken women calling themselves nurses. Physiotherapy was unknown, so the child's untreated limbs would contract and become grossly deformed and develop sores. There would be no attempt at education. Under such conditions the mind of even the most intelligent of handicapped children would deteriorate. This sort of thing was taking place only a hundred years ago. But, however shocking we may find it today, we have to recognize that the Poor Law system was an *attempt* to meet a need, and an admission that the sick poor had some right to receive organized state help, even if that help was harsh and inadequate. The aged, the spastics, the mentally ill and subnormal would certainly have starved and died if they had not received this rudimentary state help in the form of shelter and food.

In the latter half of the nineteenth century there was a movement towards Workhouse reform, led by Florence Nightingale and a Miss Twining. In 1853 Miss Twining had visited an old lady friend who had been sent into a Workhouse when she had become frail and blind, and had been terribly upset at the conditions inside. With the support of the National Association for the Promotion of Social Sciences, Florence Nightingale and Miss Twining publicized the bad conditions and urged improvements.

Finally it was decided that infirmaries for the sick poor should be set up separately from the actual Workhouse buildings. But there were many arguments regarding who would control and finance these special infirmaries. Eventually, in 1867, the Metropolitan Poor Act was passed and the Metropolitan Asylums Board was formed. This was to see to the organization of asylums for the sick poor of London. A year later a Poor Law Amendment Act gave power to the provinces to build special infirmaries for the sick poor. It was estimated that the cost of building these asylums for the poor of London would only be about £120,000, but the price of building just one infirmary, in Stepney and Poplar, was £45,000. So the buildings costs were re-estimated and it was found that the final cost was more likely to be in the region of £600,000. The Metropolitan Asylums Board, shocked at this high figure, hastily decided that it would be more economical to 'up-grade' many of the old Workhouses instead of building new separate infirmaries.

One argument for up-grading (which meant redecorating and improving old existing buildings) was that a new, separate infirmary cost a lot not only to build but also to maintain. It would be far more economical to retain all the facilities for the poor under the one roof for this meant the maintenance of only one set of kitchens, one laundry department, one heating system; and it would be easier to staff, too, because if all grades of paupers (both the sick and the able-bodied) were in one building then the laundries and the kitchens and the linen and the heating systems could be managed by unpaid able-bodied paupers who actually lived on the premises.

So, many of the old Workhouses were merely up-graded and continued to house the sick poor as they had done for years, and the fine promises of building were not fulfilled. Even as late as 1896 there were still more than 36,000 sick poor in the mixed Poor Law Workhouses and only 22,100 in separate infirmaries.

Nursing in the pauper asylums was never popular and there was always a shortage of staff, but, as a few separate new infirmaries were set up and some of the old Workhouses improved their conditions, the shortage of trained staff did lessen slightly. In

1879 an Association for Promoting Trained Nursing in Workhouses was formed, under the guidance of Miss Twining and Florence Nightingale, and by the end of the century it had trained and found jobs for more than 800 nurses in the old Workhouses and the new public infirmaries.

At the same time that concern was developing for the sick poor there was also growing public anxiety about the recurrent fever epidemics in London and other big cities. In the 1860s the inhabitants of London were constantly in danger due to widespread outbreaks of fevers. The Workhouses and the new public infirmaries and the voluntary hospitals were refusing to take people with infectious fevers, so there was a vital need for special isolation hospitals. From the 1880s onwards there was a rapid development of fever-hospital building, generally out in country areas well away from towns. By 1913 there were more than 700 fever hospitals and more than 300 smallpox hospitals in England and Wales.

So, at the start of the twentieth century several types of hospital care were available. These were mainly:

1. The voluntary hospitals which were financed by the patients and voluntary subscriptions and endowments, and which treated acutely ill 'respectable' people, i.e. the employed working classes, artisans, the new middle classes and professional people.
2. The new public hospitals and Workhouses which were financed by rates and taxes and which treated the sick poor and accommodated the chronically handicapped of the poorer classes.
3. The fever hospitals, also financed by rates and taxes.

There was also a steady growth of small 'cottage hospitals', mostly situated in rural areas and little country towns. Some of these cottage hospitals were started by local philanthropists giving legacies, and some were started by local working people who organized themselves into clubs and contributed a few pennies each week towards starting their own hospital. The cost of in-patient care was helped along by the patient paying a small fee, sometimes only a few shillings a week.

Gradually the standard of care given in some of the new public hospitals (the separate infirmaries) improved and they began to be used by acutely ill people who were not paupers. The stigma of the

Poor Law, with its emphasis on deterring public scroungers, was not so obvious when the infirmaries were separate from the main Workhouse and employed trained nurses and offered fairly good amenities. So it was not uncommon for families 'above the pauper class' to start making regular use of the new public hospitals when they needed short-term medical treatment.

The style of the late-nineteenth-century hospitals reflected the need to prevent cross-infections. The fashion was for large open wards, easily supervised by the nurses; sparse furnishing and neat wards were thought best to prevent dust and dirt; nurses' training always emphasized the need to observe strict standards of ward hygiene. Quite a lot of hospitals were built with the wards in separate single-storey blocks which provided easy access for outdoor nursing of tuberculosis patients and also served as a protection against spreading infections. Many tuberculosis patients were nursed out-of-doors all the year round.

As the twentieth century advanced the trend was for the voluntary hospitals, the big new public hospitals and the isolation hospitals to take care of the acutely ill, the infectious and the vast numbers of tuberculosis patients. What was happening to the chronically sick poor who were physically handicapped, mentally ill or subnormal, the destitute sick? Because the newest public hospitals and the voluntary hospitals were becoming increasingly selective in their choice of patients and were more interested in the acutely sick of the better classes, it was inevitable that the chronically sick poor were relegated to the original old Workhouse infirmaries where conditions did not match those in the other hospitals.

Nursing, too, in the old Workhouses remained unpopular, because the patients were chronic and there were no interesting operations or treatments to learn about. Nurses felt their skills were wasted in the day-to-day care of incurables who really only required accommodation and daily looking after. The interests of the doctors and consultants also lay mainly with the acute sick of the better social classes who could pay well, or those patients who were likely to provide some particular medical interest to themselves or their students.

During the First World War the tremendous numbers of

wounded servicemen needing hospital care and the shortage of military hospitals made a serious drain on civilian hospital resources. Whole hospitals were requisitioned by the military, and sometimes the patients were transferred to the old Workhouse infirmaries. Middle-class patients who went from their comfortable little voluntary hospitals into the Workhouse infirmaries were terribly shocked at the horrible conditions they found, for many of them had had no idea that the sick poor were being accommodated in such places.

At the end of the First World War the country's hospital services were in serious financial difficulties. There were shortages of staff and beds, and the material conditions in the hospitals had become thoroughly run down. There was a continual hazard of widespread tuberculosis, and the influenza outbreaks put an additional strain on all hospitals. In all sections of the population, young and old, military and civilian, health standards were poor and medical provision inadequate. Many civilians and soldiers were being nursed in temporary hutted hospitals.

Some of the financial difficulties of the voluntary hospitals were eased by valiant fund-raising efforts in the early 1920s. Appeals were launched, legacies were left, endowments made, and the Hospital Fête became a regular feature up and down the countryside on summer Saturdays.

During the 1920s and the early 1930s some publicity was given to criticisms of long waiting times in out-patient clinics, poor hospital food and the early waking of in-patients. Hospital journals published articles discussing these criticisms. Although no radical improvements were made, the increasing attention reflected the changing attitude towards medical care; opinion was growing that sick people had rights, they were not merely content to be the humble recipients of charity, they were beginning to want a voice in the standard of treatment they received.

In the late 1920s the position of inmates in the old Workhouse infirmaries was still bad. Ministry of Health records note that in 1928 there were 32,567 patients in separate infirmaries, and 35,864 in the general old mixed Workhouses. These inmates of the old Workhouses included adults and children who were suffering from a variety of physical and mental ills and had no home or family to care for them. Many of these old Workhouses were then well over 100 years old; they were still short of trained staff and there were insufficient bath and toilet facilities. And there was nobody specially trained to look after the young children who lived in them.

The cause of the wide difference in care was still the old reason that the acutely ill but treatable middle-class patients remained the most acceptable and popular with the medical staff of the better hospitals, whilst the unpopular hard core of chronic poor (both young and old) had the less comfortable accommodation and the less well-qualified staff because they were not medically interesting and only needed a home and daily care.

In 1929 the Local Government Act placed the administration of the Workhouses under the Local Authorities instead of the Poor Law. This meant that all the old Poor Law Workhouse infirmaries were taken over by their Local Authorities, but the change must have made little immediate difference to the vast numbers of young and old who were already in the Workhouse infirmaries. The efficiency of the take-over varied with each Authority, because some Local Authorities were very small whilst others were large and had better financial resources; and there was also a fair amount of freedom given to Local Authorities as to how much hospital provision they would make.

This freedom of the Local Authorities was highly valued, for then (as now) any hint of compulsion from central government was regarded with sheer horror as a threat to independence. The price of that much-valued freedom was paid for in terms of misery and degradation for thousands of chronically handicapped people who lacked the physical monetary independence to help themselves to a better place. For many of them the improvements, so slow in coming, never arrived in time – the aged were dead long before, and the young were too institutionalized to care any longer.

At the start of the Second World War the pattern of hospital development was very chequered, because of the many different interested bodies and the historical connections with the old Poor Laws and various voluntary charities. In the main there were:

1. The voluntary hospitals and cottage hospitals, largely sup-

ported by subscriptions and endowments and their fee-paying patients.

2. The Local Authority hospitals, some being new-built, and some being ex-Public Institutions (i.e. separate infirmaries) or ex-Metropolitan Asylums Board.

3. The old Public Institutions (Workhouse hospitals) some of which accommodated specifically mentally handicapped people.

4. The specialist hospitals, i.e. those that dealt with some specific group of people, such as children or women, or of diseases, such as cancer, fevers, tuberculosis, orthopaedic disorders, mental diseases, and so on.

5. The famous old Teaching Hospitals.

The Second World War caused a panic survey of existing hospital services because large numbers of civilian casualties were immediately expected in addition to the military wounded. Hutted temporary wards were quickly built in hospital grounds, and emergency operating theatres added. Thousands of ill in-patients were hurriedly discharged during the first few weeks of the war and whole hospitals stood practically empty awaiting the injured from bombing raids which did not immediately take place.

The war emergency meant that the Government was subsidizing and using public and private hospitals, and doctors and consultants had to work in any hospital to which they might be sent. Patients also had to go where they were sent. So, middle-class patients and their consultants from the exclusive voluntary hospitals often found themselves using the facilities of the old Workhouse infirmaries and the Local Authority hospitals; they were invariably shocked at the conditions in these big public hospitals.

The war revealed so many differences in the various hospitals that people at last realized the inequalities of medical care. It was logical that as the war approached its end plans were being finally decided on a unified system of hospital administration to be under Government control.

The formation of the National Health Service did not come easily; arguments raged about the interests of the doctors, the endowments which had been given to the voluntary hospitals, the freedom of people to be able to choose, the status of the consultants, the freedom of Local Authorities, and so on. Clubs were formed to try to preserve some of the small private hospitals, petitions were signed and heated meetings were held. The Victoria Hospital in Kingston upon Thames had extra staunch efforts made to 'save' it from the NHS: local people formed a club and contributed a few pennies every week to open a 'New Victoria' Hospital which would stay outside the NHS (years afterwards they succeeded in doing this).

However, advances in technological medicine meant that hospitals needed expensive new medical equipment and complicated apparatus; these expenses could never have been borne by all the small voluntary hospitals and, unable to maintain modern standards of care, they would eventually have become old-fashioned and third-rate. Some of the administrators of the voluntary hospitals were far-sighted enough to recognize this fact; they admitted that the voluntary hospitals had served a useful purpose but it was time for them to come under Government administration.

In July 1948 the National Health Service Act was passed; under it nearly all hospitals belonged to the nation and were to be administered by fourteen Regional Hospital Boards; only the famous old Teaching Hospitals remained partially outside the NHS system because of their links with the Universities.

After the passing of the NHS Act there was no rapid change in hospital building and organization. Improvements were slow in coming. The big old Institutions remained, and over the years they have been up-graded rather than rebuilt. The older institutions, e.g. mental or fever hospitals which had been built under the Metropolitan Asylums Board in the 1870s, tended to accommodate the aged and chronically handicapped who were socially rejected (i.e. people who lacked the resources of family or finance to ensure that their situation was more comfortable). And they still do.

There have been various scandals in recent years over the conditions in ex-Poor Law Institutions and the old Metropolitan Asylums. The book *Sans Everything* recorded that senile old people were being thoughtlessly treated in them. Peter Townsend, in his book *The Last Refuge*, drew attention to the fact that conditions in ex-Public Institutions did not match the better standards of the post-war-built Local Authority old people's Homes, and he found significantly that they catered for the socially unfortunate.

This sort of disclosure makes one suspect that the residents in institutions are 'creamed off' and that the managers of the better Homes can select the 'nicer' resident and leave the less fortunate to go to the old Institutions. This situation creates a hard core of chronic unfortunates who, like the Workhouse population of the last century, are socially and physically condemned to remain in the worst of state accommodation.

Where do chronically handicapped children fit into the structure of the National Health Service hospitals? The following section refers briefly to the function of hospitals today in relation to long-stay children.

Functions of Children's Hospitals Today

Many of the children's hospitals built at the end of the nineteenth century and the beginning of the twentieth century were sited in country districts, because their purpose was to accommodate city children who had contracted tuberculosis or fevers. Some hospitals grew from the brave tentative efforts of rich philanthropists who took sick poor children from London and actually started voluntary hospitals in their own country estates.

Children's hospitals often consisted of separate single-storey ward blocks with access to sunny courtyards, where children with tuberculosis could lie resting on their beds, out of doors day and night all the year round. In poor weather their beds would be pushed under a glass roof. Retired hospital teachers remember teaching groups of children with tuberculosis in the 1920s and 30s who lived out of doors for several years. The teachers had to wear thick boots, gloves and heavy coats to combat the cold in the winter, while in the summer they got burnt and uncomfortable in the shadeless suntrap courtyards.

After the gradual curing of tuberculosis there came a new childhood menace: poliomyelitis. The epidemics of the 1940s and 50s left large numbers of paralysed children, some of whom spent years in hospital. They were educated by visiting Local Education Authority teachers, had regular physiotherapy, were fitted with walking aids or calipers, and, if they were lucky, left the hospital at about sixteen to start some vocational training. If a child was very heavily handicapped, perhaps even still on a respirator, and had spent years out of touch with his family then he was sometimes transferred to an adult hospital at sixteen. Sometimes the adult hospital would be an old Public Assistance Institution (ex-Workhouse infirmary) accommodating the chronic sick and senile aged.

Vaccination has now almost eliminated poliomyelitis and the old long-stay children's hospitals today accommodate children who are cerebral palsied, those with spina bifida, children damaged by thalidomide, the boys with muscular dystrophy, post-road-accident victims, etc., and the mentally subnormal. One children's hospital in southern England, originally built in the late nineteenth century as a fever hospital under the Metropolitan Asylums Board, eventually became a long-stay hospital for tubercular children, followed later by poliomyelitis patients, and it now specializes in accommodating chronically physically handicapped children and mentally subnormal children. Many of these children will spend their entire childhood in hospital.

In long-stay hospitals children receive all the surgical treatment, drugs and physiotherapy they need: they are provided with physical aids (wheel-chairs, calipers, mechanical limbs) and taught how to use them; and they are educated under the administration of the local education authority Special Education departments.

Why is it ever necessary for children to be long-stay in-patients? Why cannot handicapped children remain in their own homes (or go to Residential Special Schools) and only attend hospitals on an out-patient basis for their treatment? Or, if they *have* to receive surgery and in-patient care, why cannot their hospital stay be kept short?

The reason is that many children get caught up in some problem that risks their becoming totally hospitalized. It is all too easy for handicapped children to become part of the hospital system and sometimes very difficult to extricate them from it. One conflicting problem is that the law says a child must receive education, so, if he is handicapped and there is a shortage of Special

Schools and he can be educated in a children's hospital at the same time as receiving help with aids, physiotherapy, and so on, then he will stay as an in-patient while he waits for a place in a Special School. If the Special School waiting list is long he may not be considered as an urgent case for a place (because he is already receiving education); therefore he might spend many years as an in-patient. Other children never even get on a list for a Special School, but stay all their schooldays in the hospital and get transferred to an adult Home or hospital when they are sixteen.

Other reasons for children staying in hospitals for years may be housing problems, illness in the family, the loss of one or both parents, the attempted suicide of mother, the break-up of the marriage, the imprisonment of a parent, a large family and mother's inability to cope also with a heavily handicapped child, or because the child has been rejected or abandoned.

So, what is the function of children's hospitals today? First, it is to give purely *hospital care*. This covers operations, for instance for children with spina bifida, cerebral palsy, hip and spinal defects. It also covers physiotherapy, e.g. children with cerebral palsy need physiotherapy in order to prevent deformities in their limbs, and children damaged by thalidomide need to be taught how to manage their mechanical aids. Hospital care also means regulation of drugs, as in epilepsy and asthma, medical tests, X-rays, physical and mental observations and control of diet.

These special functions of modern hospitals are accepted for we know that these are specialist fields which inevitably mean in-patient care. But, a second, and less well-known function of children's hospitals is that relating to *social aid*, a function which exists today just as much as it did 100 years ago when the Workhouses were crammed with the chronically handicapped and homeless poor. Social aid for a handicapped child may mean admitting him to hospital because of his social problem connected with housing and/or family.

A handicapped child in a family that is already under some strain may be the 'last straw' in a situation that is fast becoming intolerable, and it is here that the hospital personnel can step in and admit a child purely in order to ease the family strain. Sometimes such care is short-term, perhaps while the family moves house or takes a much-needed holiday. Sometimes it is long-term, meaning an entire childhood will be spent in hospital. Sometimes it *begins* with the intention of being only short-term but circumstances lead to it becoming long-term care.

The following stories show how easy it is for a child to become hospitalized because of social reasons.

D.R. was aged eighteen months when he was admitted to hospital; he was cerebral palsied and also had a congenital deformity of the hips. Mother had been trying to cope with three small children in a caravan, and father was out of work. D.R. was admitted to hospital primarily for hip corrections and physiotherapy, but the housing problem and mother's need to go to work resulted in his remaining in hospital. He spent nearly two years in an orthopaedic ward, surrounded by children who were in cots and undergoing traction or plaster treatments; D.R. used to move about the ward in a little flat trolley on wheels. He rarely saw his mother as getting transport to the country hospital was difficult, and anyway she was at work most of the day. From the orthopaedic ward D.R. was transferred to a cerebral palsy unit in the same hospital, where there was a nursery class. Because of the long waiting list for a placement in a Residential Special School which he needed, and because the family's problems did not improve, D.R. remained in hospital for four years altogether, from the age of eighteen months until nearly six. During that time his family contact became almost non-existent. Only the efforts of a Local Authority social worker during his last six months in hospital managed to get the family in contact with him again. Today D.R. is in a Residential Special School run by a Voluntary Society, his family has got a house and father has a job, and D.R. spends all the school holidays with his family. But for four years his home was a hospital, solely because of social reasons.

Q.B. was aged four when his mother had a breakdown. The breakdown was caused partly by the serious physical and mental handicap of Q. The family doctor, faced with the sudden problem of mother's illness and Q.'s situation, contacted the hospital which

Q. attended as an out-patient for physiotherapy. The hospital immediately arranged for temporary admission for Q. until his mother was better. However, it was soon realized that, even when mother was better, Q.B. would never be entirely received back into the family. He was put on the waiting list for a Residential Special School run by a Voluntary Society. The waiting list was very long but he eventually received a place. Now, whenever the school closes for holidays Q. is sent back into the hospital because the family still will not accept him and there is nowhere else for him to go. He is not incontinent, he can feed himself and dress himself and talk, but he has physical and mental handicaps. His initial admittance to hospital was on a short-term emergency basis for social reasons but it resulted in four years as a hospital in-patient and the frequent re-admittance for school holidays.

B.B. was aged seven, and was the middle child of a large family whose mother had left them. The four brothers and sisters were taken into the care of their Local Authority Children's Department and sent to a Village Home for children in care. The Village would not take B.B. because she had a physical handicap, and the Local Authority ruling was that handicapped children were not to be sent there. B.B.'s handicap was a very slight limp, she was not in a wheel-chair, she was of average intelligence, perfectly able to care for herself and very healthy. The only place that could be found for her was the hospital that she had attended for physiotherapy as an out-patient. She was able to receive education in the hospital school, so the arrangement was perfectly satisfactory to her Local Education Authority. She remained in the hospital, living in a ward, for more than three years. She finally managed to get a place in a Residential Special School for physically handicapped children that was run by a Voluntary Society. She was always very resentful that she had been separated from her brothers and sisters, and was always talking of the days when 'dad will get us a new mummy and we can all go home again'. The administrative machinery that would not allow B.B. to be accommodated in the Village Home because of her slight handicap did not take into account the poverty of the hospital environment and the strain of the family separation they condemned B.B. to endure

The main types of Hospital Care for Children In-patients

	Hospitals which admit acutely ill children for short-stay* in-patient care (majority will include adults)	Hospitals admitting physically ill or disabled children for medium-* or long-stay* in-patient care (majority will be for children only although some of the specialist hospitals, e.g. orthopaedic hospitals, may include adults)	Hospitals which admit mentally ill or mentally subnormal children for medium or long-stay care (these hospitals may include adults)
TYPE OF HOSPITAL AND ITS HISTORICAL BACKGROUND	Ex-voluntary hospitals Ex-cottage hospitals Teaching hospitals and teaching hospital branches Ex-separate Poor Law infirmaries and ex-Metropolitan Asylums Board and Local Authority hospitals (now usually described as District General Hospitals) Post-war-built District Hospitals Hospitals for special diseases (e.g. cancer) Hospitals for children only	Teaching hospital branches (mainly situated in country areas) Ex-Metropolitan Asylums Board fever and tuberculosis Board (mainly in country areas) Hospitals for special diseases (e.g., chest, orthopaedic care)	Ex-Poor Law infirmaries Ex-Metropolitan Asylums Board hospitals (built specially for the mentally ill and the mentally subnormal in the last part of the nineteenth century) Ex-fever hospitals
TYPE OF DISORDER ADMITTED	Acute illness, e.g. appendicitis, pneumonia, road and other accidents, acute polio, acute meningitis, cystic fibrosis, heart diseases, spina bifida for surgical treatments, other surgical treatments, blood disorders, asthma, new-born-baby illnesses, etc.	Long-term illnesses and incurable physical disabilities, e.g. cerebral palsy, muscular dystrophy, spina bifida, post-polio., post-meningitis, congenital limb and spine disabilities, blood diseases rheumatism, post-road accidents and post- other accidents, asthma, cystic fibrosis, etc.	*Mental illnesses:* depressions, phobias, anxieties, obsessions, schizophrenia, autism, epilepsy, maladjustment, etc. (may be short, long, or medium stay) *Mental subnormality:* autism, schizophrenia, mongolism, idiocy, imbecility, epilepsy, brain damage, and physically handicapped children who are also mentally subnormal, e.g. spastics (most of these groups will be long-stay)

CARE NEEDED AND GIVEN	Medical and/or surgical treatment of an immediate short-term nature	Medical and/or surgical treatment Long-term home accommodation	Medical treatment, e.g. drugs; psychotherapy; sometimes surgical treatment and e.c.t. Long-term home accommodation
EDUCATIONAL PROVISION	Bedside teaching by qualified teachers employed by the Local Education Authority under the Department of Education and Science	Ward and schoolroom teaching by qualified teachers employed by Local Education Authorities and under the Department of Education and Science	Ward and schoolroom teaching, with teachers employed by the LEA under the Department of Education and Science.
SOCIAL PROBLEMS AS A REASON FOR ADMITTANCE	Unlikely to be a prime reason for admittance to an acute short-stay type of hospital. Should a social problem occur during or following treatment then the child may be transferred to a long-stay hospital	A social problem would be a frequent reason for admission to any of these hospitals. The problems would include: housing, family disturbance, family illness, lack of family, rejection; or it may be due to poor community facilities, e.g. no schools, no day hospitals, no training centres, no aid for the families	

*Short-stay is up to three months as an in-patient.
Medium-stay is between three months and two years.
Long-stay is two years or longer.
(Department of Health and Social Security definition: Eileen Brook)

for three years; it was sufficient satisfaction to them that the administrative rules had been observed.

T.S. spent more than three years in hospital because of the inability of her mother to cope with a young handicapped child. Father had left the family, mother was in a high flat, and there were two other small children. T.S. was an over-active child, difficult to manage in a small confined home. Her admittance to hospital at the age of three was in order to save mother from a complete breakdown; had this occurred then the other children would have had to go into Care. T.S. did not need hospital treatment, apart from physiotherapy; she was physically handicapped but could feed herself and was of average intelligence. During her time in hospital, T.S.'s link with her family became less and less, she was never visited and did not go home for holidays. Eventually her feelings of rejection resulted in her becoming emotionally distressed and maladjusted. Her hospital stay was also prolonged because attempts to get her into a Residential Special School for Physically Handicapped Children were thwarted by a shortage of Special School places and the selection procedures at some schools which meant that she was turned down on grounds of difficult behaviour.

The need for education is sometimes the *sole* reason for a child going to a long-stay hospital. He may have a perfectly happy home and united family, but it is impossible to find a school for him. This is particularly so if a child has more than one handicap, and a hospital which has a school may be the only answer. This was the reason for R.N. going to a long-stay hospital. She was deaf and cerebral palsied and educationally retarded, but not subnormal. She was already six and had not received any education or training for her deafness. The family lived in a country district where there were no facilities for R.N. Eventually she was admitted to a children's hospital 200 miles away from her home. The family was pathetically grateful when the hospital staff promised to do all they could to find a school for R.N. In the hospital R.N. received Infant School activities, and had special periods each week for deaf education. Her family missed her painfully, and she also fretted for them. She spent two years in that hospital before finally getting a place in a Residential Special School for children with multiple handicaps. The school was actually run by another Local Education Authority than R.N.'s own and was still 200 miles away from the family home. The only reason that R.N. had to live for two years in a long-stay hospital was the inadequate Special Education provisions in her own Local Authority.

E.S. was another child whose family were united and happy. She was physically handicapped and mentally retarded, and spent twelve years in a hospital more than 200 miles away from her home and family because she could receive education and physiotherapy in that hospital, and there was no school near her home. Her family ties remained strong even during those twelve long years away from home; now she is in a Voluntary Society Home for Handicapped Adults near her home.

So, a common, perhaps not well-known, function of children's hospitals today is that they not only give conventional hospital care, but they also *provide accommodation* for the chronically, physically and/or mentally handicapped child with family, housing or Special School placement problems.

The Development of Special Education

The education of handicapped children in the nineteenth century was largely pioneered by Voluntary Societies interested in the training of blind, deaf-and-dumb, epileptic, or 'idiotic' children, their work being influenced by the educational theories of Jean Itard and Edouard Seguin, and later on by Maria Montessori. From the early beginnings, which mainly concentrated on giving the children some useful 'training', a rather complicated three-tier system of state, Independent and Voluntary Society provision of Special Education has developed; it caters for the education of the blind, deaf, the educationally subnormal, the delicate, the maladjusted, the physically handicapped and the multiply handicapped; there are schools which cater especially for spastics or for children with spina bifida, asthma or speech problems. Some Special Schools are residential; others are day schools and the children may go daily by transport provided by their Local Authority. In 1967 over 90,000 children were receiving some form of Special Education, either in Day or Residential Schools, or in Special Classes, or through Home Teachers; there were also over 14,000 children waiting for admission to Special Schools.

The provision of Special Education is much better in some areas than in others. Local Authorities have a fair degree of freedom regarding how much Special Education they provide, according to their estimates of the needs of their school population. If a Local Authority cannot provide a place in its own district for a handicapped child then it may pay for the child to attend a Voluntary Society School, either in or out of their area, or to attend a Special School belonging to another Local Authority. A Local Authority may pay as much as £1,000 a year for a child to attend a Voluntary Society Residential Special School. If it were not for the Voluntary Society Special Schools there would be many more children in long-stay hospitals; e.g. one Society has five Residential Schools for severely physically handicapped children and takes more than 200 children; another has nine Schools and places for more than 500. The expenses of these Schools are considerable, one Society estimates that staffing salaries for nine Schools was as high as £483,000 in 1969–70 (this included salaries of teachers, therapists, domestics, etc.). Apart from the payment made for individual children by Local Authorities, these Voluntary Society Schools depend entirely on voluntary subscriptions. Voluntary Societies have a fine history of pioneering work for the handicapped, e.g. the work of the Spastics Society in research and the education of cerebral palsied children has been outstanding, and has resulted in that Society providing a higher standard of all-round care than that offered by the state to any one special group of handicapped people.

The Development of Child-Care Services

Local Authority Children's Departments were developed after the Second World War, partly because wartime evacuation had revealed many home problems affecting children, and partly because a scandal had occurred when a fostered child was ill-treated and died. In 1945 the Home Office appointed a Committee, under the Chairmanship of Myra Curtis, which investigated the whole question of child care, with particular references to fostering and all Children's Homes, e.g. Voluntary Society Orphanages, Local Authority Homes, private Homes and Workhouses. The Committee completed its report in 1946, and recommended that Local Authorities should each form a Children's Department, with a Children's Officer in charge and a staff of Child Care Officers. The staff of these Children's Departments, who would eventually have professional training, would supervise fostering and all types of Children's Homes, and also give advice and help to families with problems related to children and people who wished to adopt. All Voluntary Society and private Homes would have to be registered; and foster homes and Local Authority Homes, Voluntary Society and private Homes, would have to be regularly inspected by Child Care staff to ensure that they provided the children with approved living conditions and proper care. These important recommendations were incorporated into the resulting 1948 Children's Act.

This first Children's Act thus made sure that no substitute Home could take a child into its care and then deprive him of what he needed as a growing, vulnerable and sensitive being, that is affection and understanding, a pleasant environment, play space and toys, books, recreation in the form of outings and holidays, and a good standard of clothing, toilet and bath facilities. But, despite the fact that many handicapped children were living in hospitals, being permanently or temporarily apart from their families, the Act did not legislate that hospitalized children should come specifically under the protection of the Local Authority Children's Departments. So, whilst a Children's Home in a district would have to be registered, and could be rigorously inspected by the Local Authority Child Care Officers, there might still be a children's long-stay hospital a few miles away where children would spend an entire childhood in very limited conditions; nothing in the Children's Act gave the Local Authority Children's Officer legislative powers to investigate and take proceedings against a hospital which did not comply with the standards of child care required by the Home Office. This situation was surprising in view of the fact that the Curtis Committee, in its inspections of Homes, Hostels, Schools, and so on, had made definite mention of a hospital where children '... had nothing and looked bored.... A young nurse was in charge and did not seem much interested in discussing the welfare or occupations of the children.... These children had little of occupational or social interest after the teacher left at three o'clock in the afternoon....' Again, after a visit to a Sanitorium they reported that 'there was an obvious need for some form of occupation to fill the gap between the limited hours of schoolroom education and the children's long hours of entire leisure which the few nurses could not hope to deal with. The children seemed to have few toys and little or no materials for play or handiwork; they were bored and listless.'

Nearly a quarter of a century has passed since the Curtis Committee published its report, and children in long-stay hospitals are still 'bored and listless' and there are still young nurses 'not much interested'. There have been other Children's Acts since 1948, but each new bit of legislation brought in to protect children always leaves hospital inspection out of its recommendations. Perhaps this is due to the prestige that the medical professions enjoy in this country; they appear to be the undisputed experts on a variety of subjects not connected with medicine, one of which is, unfortunately, child care.

Part Two
Children in Hospitals

Introduction

There are two related aspects of child care. First, there is the physical care of the child: his feeding, sleeping, toileting, dressing and undressing routines; the environment, and the ways in which standards of physical care affect his existence as a dependent child. Secondly, there is the more subtle 'mother-care' aspect of child care, which influences the child's contentment and confidence, his occupations, the attention paid to him, his social and intellectual development, and his existence as an independent individual. The combination of these two aspects of child care complete 'home-making' in a residential institution.

During the course of visiting various establishments which cared for handicapped children, it was noticed that certain differences existed in the home-making practices according to whether the organization was directed by Local Authorities, hospitals or Voluntary Societies. It was obvious that the Schools and Homes aimed at certain standards of care commensurate with normal family life, but the hospitals did not. This raised the question of *why* Residential Schools and Homes gave children a better standard of child care than the hospitals did. In order to understand what actually takes place in institutions which care for handicapped children, some detailed observations were made in four places.

It was decided to observe the life of the children during the week-ends, because this would be a time when they would be free of school routines, and entirely in the charge of nurses or houseparents; and, assuming that the nurses and houseparents (unlike the teachers) would have some duties concerned with the domestic running of the establishment, then it might be seen how the children fitted into domestic routines when not having school. Particular attention was paid to standards of mothering and home-making, which included daily routines, the communication between staff and children, occupations and play, socialization, the physical environment of the institutions, and the behaviour of the children.

The following diaries record the week-end lives of some handicapped children and give a brief glimpse of what it is like to be a small child in an institution.

1. Fieldway: a Residential School in the Country

Fieldway was organized and financed by a Voluntary Society. It was in a country district, surrounded by woods and farmlands, poorly served by public transport and some distance from shops or town. It accommodated fifty-three boys and girls, aged from five to sixteen. All the children were cerebral palsied and educationally subnormal. Some had additional handicaps, such as epilepsy, speech disorders, perception disabilities and behaviour problems. Seven children were very deaf. Eight needed help with feeding, and most of them needed aid with dressing and toileting. They used artificial aids for walking (sticks, calipers) or had wheel-chairs. Several were totally handicapped, having no speech and needing help with everything. Some of the children had family problems, e.g. family illness or breakdown, or loss of family contact.

The house, and combined school-wing, was a large converted Manor House at the end of a long drive. There was an open playing space in front of the porch, and behind the house there was a playground with swings and slides and a small stone ornamental play-house and lawns and gardens. Amongst the trees was a little 'adventure playground' consisting of an old rowing boat and some ropes hanging from trees.

In the hall was a wide staircase and a lift, and an adjoining cloakroom where outdoor clothes were stored. The children used the hall as a lounge and were able to play, read, write letters or watch the arrival of visitors and tradespeople as they sat there. There was nearly always a small group of children there; it was furnished with a large settee, an armchair and a coffee-table, carpeting covered the floor, a book-shelf had flowers on it and pictures were on the walls.

Leading from the hall was a large playroom/lounge, which

was furnished with carpeting, armchairs, a settee, a piano and television set, curtains, pictures and a large mattress on the floor. The children also had access to the school hall, at the end of a small corridor, where they played with large apparatus such as train sets. This hall had a raised stage at one end.

The dining-room was at the end of another small corridor, it had twelve separate tables and a serving-hatch led from the kitchen.

There were four downstairs bedrooms for boys, and six upstairs bedrooms for girls and the younger boys. There were three main bathrooms, nine baths, fifteen toilets and three showers, some being upstairs and some downstairs.

The schoolrooms were on the other side of the buildings and were not used during the week-ends. The children were free to go into the playroom/lounge, the big school-hall, the hall/lounge, their bedrooms and the gardens. The gardens were continually used, but for safety's sake the children were not allowed to go too far down the long drive if unaccompanied. The paths round the back of the house and leading past staff houses were used for cycling. The woods were used for wood-collecting and blackberrying. The play-space in front of the entrance porch was used for organized games.

Children who could manage the stairs were encouraged to do so; the wheel-chair children went up by the lift.

All the rooms in Fieldway had gay patterned curtains and wallpapers, and carpets were in all rooms except the dining-room and school hall. There were framed pictures on the walls, flowers decorated every room and the hall, and the paint-work was fresh and bright.

Each bedroom had one or two wardrobes, low wooden-headed divans, and attractive counterpanes. The beds were arranged at angles. Every bedroom had wash-basins and mirrors fixed into the wall above the basins, and toothbrush and mugholders were in wall-attachments by the mirrors. Towels and flannels hung on a mobile towel rail. The children kept their hair-brushes and some personal belongings in their wooden lockers beside their beds. Other toys and personal possessions were kept on top of the lockers, in the wardrobe or on the wide window-sills. The older girls had more sophisticated make-up tables in their bedrooms.

The number of children sharing a bedroom varied from three to seven. Some of the older boys slept four in a room, in bunk-beds. It was usual for the younger children to sleep six or seven to a room, whilst the older ones were kept to three or four. The bedrooms were each given the name of a flower or tree, and they all showed differences according to the children's ages, sex and interests: there were soft toys in some, newspaper cuttings in others, powder and cosmetics, photographs, notepaper and books or hobbies in others.

The children were able to go to the toilets whenever they wished. Some toilets were in the bathrooms, screened off by curtains or wooden partitions, others were in separate cloakrooms, containing hand-basins and towels as well. It was part of general routine that the children used the toilets before breakfast, after breakfast, before lunch and after lunch, if necessary, and before going to bed.

Eating arrangements at Fieldway had three to five children at each table; the children always kept to their own places. They were grouped according to age and the amount of help they needed with feeding, and a houseparent sat at the table with the children who needed help. Nearly all the children required some supervision when eating, because of their heavy handicaps; some needed special spoons or straws. About four or five children who were obese sat together at one table, in order to make their low-calorie diet easier to bear.

As the food was cooked in the adjoining kitchen, the children were well aware of the chore of cooking and were familiar with cooking smells and home-made food. Although the staff did not eat their own meals with the children, their dining-room adjoined the children's dining-room and they could be seen eating.

The dining-tables were laid for the children with mats, side-plates, serving utensils, water-jugs and glasses, and vegetable dishes. The children helped themselves to vegetables, water or orange juice, or bread, as required. At tea and breakfast, the children had jugs of tea on the table, to which they helped themselves or each other. When they arrived in the dining-room they usually had pinafores put on, or were given their napkin squares.

Soiled napkins or pinafores were put into a basket at the end of the meal. The older girls and boys helped in serving the meals and in clearing away afterwards. Grace was said at the start of the meal; children did not leave the dining-room until all, or nearly all, of the children had finished eating. Mealtimes were always peaceful, unhurried and sociable occasions. The dining-room was never used for any other purpose except eating.

Personal visitors and families were allowed to visit Fieldway schoolchildren as they wished. They could also spend week-ends at home whenever they wished. Voluntary visitor/helpers came from nearby places to help with outings at the week-ends, e.g. the local Rotary and Lions' Club, and the 'Friends' of the School. Every Sunday a nearby boys' public school sent volunteers either to help take the children to Church, or to wheel them up and down the drive and play with them in the house and gardens. Members of staff sometimes took the children out to tea in the town, and the matron took two deaf girls out to tea with her during one week-end I spent at the school. Sometimes, a houseparent would take a child home with her when she had an afternoon off.

The rambling size of Fieldway School made it easy for visitors to get away from other children or staff when they visited their own children. They could go to the bedrooms, or find a corner in one of the downstairs rooms, or in the grounds if the weather was dry.

Staff

There were thirteen housemothers and two housefathers; some of these houseparents had been working at the school for at least five years. The headmistress had the overall responsibility for running the school and the house, but teachers were not on duty during week-ends. Sometimes one or two student houseparents were in the school for several months, completing practical work for their courses. Houseparents were usually qualified, with Home Office Certificates in Residential Child Care; others had completed courses of training in child care under the training scheme organized by the Voluntary Society which ran the school. There was also a matron (a qualified nurse), cooks and domestic staff.

Houseparents did not usually have days off during week-ends. They had 3½ hours off during a Saturday and Sunday, in the early afternoon or during part of the morning or late afternoon.

Each bedroom had its own housemother or father, and that houseparent would stay with a group of children until they got older and moved into another bedroom. Houseparents started their morning at 7.30 a.m., with getting the children up out of bed, dressed, washed and down to breakfast. Their duties finished when the children went to bed: lights-out for the younger ones was between 7 p.m. and 7.30 p.m., and for the older children at about 9 p.m.

The houseparents' duties consisted of looking after the children during play activities, organizing play and games indoors and outside; caring for clothing, washing fine clothes and underwear, ironing, mending; tidying up bedrooms and playrooms; making beds, seeing to bed-linen; helping with feeding and serving of meals; making the big open fire in the playroom/lounge; caring for wheel-chairs, tricycles, toys, play materials; toileting, bathing, helping with dressing and undressing; and helping with letter-writing, telephoning parents, making contact with visitors or coping with homesickness or behaviour problems.

The vast amount of ironing was often done during the night (by the night-duty houseparent). The night-duty houseparent did not have to get the children up, nor did she have any duties connected with breakfast or making beds. Her main task was to see that the children were settled during the night, to see to night-toileting as necessary, and to make sure that all was safe from fire.

Diary of a Week-end

Anna, aged eight, was cerebral palsied and mentally limited; she needed help with dressing, going to the lavatory, and bathing; she could not walk, but could slowly crawl on her hands and knees, and she had a wheel-chair.

Peter, aged seven, had a complicated athetoid type of cerebral palsy. He was very severely handicapped, being unable to walk or crawl, hold anything or feed himself. He also had a severe speech disability. He could be described as 'totally handicapped' because he needed help with everything. His achievements were so limited by his physical handicaps that he functioned as a mentally retarded child, but in reality he may *not* have been very dull.

Jimmy, aged six, was cerebral palsied, and unable to walk or stand, but he could crawl and pull himself up on to the edge of a table or chair. He had a wheel-chair, and could ride a tricycle with his feet fastened in pedal-straps. He needed help and supervision when toileting, dressing and bathing. He was mentally retarded, and also had behaviour problems.

Saturday

Between 8.30 and 9.30 a.m.: Anna and Peter had their breakfast in the dining-hall. Then Anna was dressed in a warm coat, woollen hat and gloves, and went in the garden in her wheel-chair. Peter was taken to the lavatory, where he was supported by his housemother. Then he had his hands washed.

Between 9.45 and 12 a.m.: Anna played a ball game in the garden, with a group of six other children. The game was organized by two housemothers and it consisted of rolling balls on to a target and throwing balls into a bucket that stood in the middle of their circle of wheel-chairs. The children needed a lot of help because some were unable to control their hands or feet, so the houseparents held their limbs as they pushed against the ball. As they played, a drink of hot chocolate was brought out to them. Some of the children needed help with drinking, and could manage only with a polythene straw. Anna managed her own drink.

Peter stayed indoors, in the lounge, where there was a fire burning. There were about twelve children in the lounge and they wanted to play a game, so three houseparents arranged the children into a circle. One houseparent worked the record-player and they played 'musical hat', 'miaow' and 'articles with wheels'. Some of the children who took part were as badly handicapped as Peter, some less. In 'musical hat' the very handicapped children were helped by the houseparents actually passing the hat for them;

the houseparents had to run very quickly from child to child in order to get round the circle to the music, and this provoked much laughter from the children and adults. When the hot drinks came into the lounge Peter had to be supported and helped as he always had difficulty in swallowing and sucking.

After drinks, a small week-old black lamb was brought into the lounge by a farm-worker from the adjoining estate. He put the lamb by the grate and the children gathered round to look at it. Peter was laid on the floor by the lamb and his hands were held on to the lamb's back so that he could touch the thick curly coat; he laughed, pleased by the feel of the lamb. When the lamb had been taken outside again Peter had a long period sitting on one of the housefathers' laps, in an armchair in front of the fire, listening to records.

Meanwhile, some of the other children in the room made a 'house' with a huge blanket draped over three armchairs and a table, cushions and a mattress were put underneath, and about six children got inside. They explained that the gaps by the armchairs were their 'front and back doors'. Now and again a housemother crawled inside the house and pretended to eat a cake or drink tea from an imaginary cup. Peter was lifted in there and he lay smiling on the mattress, the crawling children taking care not to kick him in the face with their heavy boots.

At 12 Anna, who had been for a push down the drive after finishing her ball game, was taken indoors and she started getting ready for lunch. As there were a lot of toilets in the building and not all the children started getting ready for lunch at the same time, Anna did not have to wait for a lavatory to be vacant. There were no other children in the toilet with Anna, and the housemother left her to wash her hands on her own, whilst she went to help somebody else. The wash-basin was quite low, and Anna could manage easily as she sat in her wheel-chair.

Peter was put into his tip-up wheel-chair and taken to the lavatory to have his hands washed. He had to wait for five minutes outside the lavatory because two boys were already in there. After he had finished he was wheeled beside the handbasin, and it was filled with water so that he could dangle his hands in the water and splash up and down with the soap.

At 12.15 p.m. Anna and Peter were wheeled into the dining-hall. They were put into their usual places and had their feeder-bibs put on. Anna was the first child to arrive at her table, and she played with the side-plates and sweet spoons as she waited for the others.

At 12.30 p.m.: All the children were in, and Grace was said. Peter had to be fed by the housemother sitting on a small chair beside him at his table; she also helped to feed another child at the same table. Anna helped herself to vegetables from the dish that was in the centre of his table, and she also served one of the other, more handicapped, children at her table. Serving vegetables was quite difficult for Anna, but, apart from spilling some bits of potato, she managed very well.

At 1.30 p.m.: Lunch was over, and the children began to move out of the dining-room. Peter was taken up to his bedroom and his housemother cleaned his teeth for him and then put him on his bed to rest. Anna shared Peter's bedroom. She was given her toothbrush, flannel and towel and left to clean her teeth and wash her hands and face at the little hand-basin. She stared at her face, with a very serious expression, for about ten minutes, in the mirror above the basin.

Anna and Peter then rested on their beds until about 2.30.

From 2.30 until 4.45 p.m.: Peter was taken to the lavatory after he got up from rest, and then he went downstairs in the lift, and was wheeled into the lounge. During the afternoon he alternated between sitting on his housefather's lap (the same houseparent who had cared for him during the morning play-period) and being propped up in the fireside armchair on his own. Most of the time he listened to records, and two or three other children listened with him. Other children played in the blanket house they had made before lunch; some played cards, knitted or were helped to write letters. At one point the record-player broke, and the house-father had to take it to pieces; Peter was laid on the floor so that he could watch this operation.

Anna spent some time downstairs in the hall/lounge, playing cards with two other older children. There was a lot of giggling and shouting of 'snap' and the cards kept falling on the floor. After a while Anna went out in the garden in her wheel-chair, and then some of the housemothers pushed her and five other children up the drive for a little walk. One boy was taken to the cake-shop, at the end of the drive and across the main road, to get some cakes for tea. When the children came back from their walk, they went into the lounge and sat round the fire. Meanwhile, in the big recreation hall a small group of children were playing with constructional train sets.

At 4.45 p.m.: The children got ready for early supper. Peter was carried to the lavatory and had his hands washed, and Anna was wheeled into a small toilet down the corridor and left on her own to wash her hands and dry them on the roller towel. Her housemother fetched her after about five minutes. All the children were in the dining-room by 5 p.m.

From 5 until 6 p.m.: The children were having supper. Anna helped herself to bread and butter and slices of cake, and poured her own tea from the jug on her table. Pouring was difficult, but she was allowed to try and nobody interfered with her. The main course was a cooked snack. Peter had a cake with his supper, which had been bought for him by the child who had gone down to the cake-shop earlier in the afternoon. This child, who shared Peter's bedroom, was his special friend.

At 6 p.m.: Supper was over and Anna went up in the lift to her bedroom to get ready for bed. She was not hurried at all; she washed herself at one of the two little hand-basins in the bedroom, spending a lot of time peering at herself in the mirror and rubbing hard at her neck with the soap and flannel. She was encouraged to undress herself as much as possible but she did have some help. The other five children of her bedroom (Peter amongst them) were also getting ready for bed, either undressing or trying to wash themselves. Part of the time, another houseparent looked into the room and helped a little as Anna's housemother was in the bathroom bathing one of the children. The school matron also looked round to see if all was going smoothly. Peter, being so helpless, had to be undressed and toileted by his housemother; but, for a little while, he was put in front of one of the bedroom wash-basins and dabbled his hands in the water on his own, squeezing out his flannel a little in his clenched fists, and looking at himself in the mirror.

By 6.30 p.m.: Peter was in bed with a soft toy at his side. Anna was in her nightdress and dressing gown. She had been encouraged by her housemother to fold up her clothes and put them in a neat pile at the end of her bed. She then played for a little while on the bedroom floor; she had a doll. Three of the other children of that room were also playing on the floor, with puzzles, books and dolls.

At 7 p.m.: Anna was taken to the lavatory for the last time. All the children were then tucked down into bed, given a 'goodnight' cuddle by the housemother, and the light was put out.

Sunday

At 8.15 a.m.: The children were still in bed. They had been given a lie-in because the clocks had been put forward the night before and they had 'lost' an hour. Normally they were roused at 7.30 a.m. by their housemothers, who went into the bedrooms and drew the curtains and called them to 'wake up'. The night-duty houseparent, who always did this job, did not have any duties connected with getting the children up in the mornings. Her responsibilities were to attend to children who were ill or having disturbed nights; she usually spent her time on the landing nearest the bedrooms of the younger children, and sometimes she did a pile of ironing. Matron was always on call if necessary. On this particular Sunday, which was very cold and frosty, Jimmy was already awake and playing quietly on his bed with a teddy bear when his housemother went into the bedroom. The curtains were still drawn across, and the room was dim and quiet and some of the other children were still asleep. Jimmy shared this bedroom with five other children, including Anna and Peter.

Between 8.30 and 9.30 a.m.: All the children were getting up and ready for breakfast. Jimmy washed and dressed himself as much as possible without help. He was a long time dressing since he was inclined to busy himself with other things and interfere with other children; he needed repeated reminders to get ready, although he was not hurried or grumbled at. He played with his locker and chatted about a framed picture of an elephant that hung on the wall opposite his bed. The picture was his own, having been painted for him by a friend of the staff. When he was dressed his housemother wheeled him along to the lavatory.

Elsewhere in the house the other children were getting up, the severely handicapped ones being lifted, dressed and washed by their houseparents. The older girls and boys bathed or showered in the mornings, some needing a lot of assistance from staff. The younger children (aged six to twelve) were washed in their bedrooms as they usually had a bath at night-time. The children all cleaned their teeth after washing. They kept their toothbrushes in the wall-attachments above the handbasins and the brushes were not named as they were all very individual – perhaps having Noddy or animal faces on them, or being distinctive colours. Most of the children also had their own toothpaste, which they kept in their tooth-mugs.

On the landing there was quite a bustle and noise, as older girls moved along in their dressing-gowns to and from the bathrooms and shower-rooms, or as they tidied up their bedrooms. Downstairs, the older boys were equally busy. All children over fourteen were responsible (if physically capable) for tidying up their own bedrooms.

At 9.30 a.m.: It was breakfast time. The tables had already been laid with side-plates, bread and butter, utensils and fruit. Some of the children played with the side-plates and cutlery as they waited for breakfast to start, and utensils were occasionally dropped on the floor. Houseparents were still busy bringing children into the dining-room and putting on feeders and going back for more children coming down in the lift. The kitchen staff could be seen through the serving hatch, waiting to dish up breakfast.

Grace was said before breakfast started, and, as the children started to eat, the room became very quiet and peaceful. Able children poured their own drinks and helped themselves to bread and butter. Some food was spilt on the floor as the more heavily handicapped children tried to manage on their own. Jimmy had breakfast at a table with four other children, two of whom needed feeding, and one housemother sat at the table. Jimmy fed himself, poured drinks for the other children, and helped to hand round the bread and butter.

All the children had finished breakfast by 10.15 and they left the dining-room.

Between 10.15 and 12.15: It was play period. First of all, some of the children went to the lavatories. Afterwards, they went into the lounge or the big recreation hall. A small group of children, consisting of three older girls, a very handicapped teenage boy, and two little boys aged eight, sat in the hall/lounge. The older boy drew pictures on a pad and the others watched him; he drew by holding a felt-pen in his bare foot; he could not speak or use his hands.

There were other groups of children scattered through the house and garden. Some children were in their wheel-chairs just outside the front door, playing ball games, the heavily handicapped children receiving a lot of aid from houseparents. One small group played in the adventure playground, pretending they were rowing along on a river. Three boys went off on their tricycles, looking at staff cars; then they decided to go round the corner by the farm, to look for wood for the lounge fire. One of these three boys came rushing back shortly afterwards, in great excitement at having found a dead bird. He had placed the bird, long-dead and desiccated, carefully in his saddle-bag. He went, as quickly as his handicap allowed, into the house and showed it to his houseparent, saying: 'I must bury it.'

The other children gathered round in sympathetic interest. He went to a flower bed just outside the front door, scratched a hole, with a wobbly foot, and put the bird in the shallow hole and covered it with earth. Two other boys then joined him and all three went eagerly away to look for more dead birds.

Collecting wood was also taking place in the woods. This was an activity which went on with enthusiasm all through the winter. Small logs and sticks were stacked in boxes and dragged to the back door of the house, or stored in a little shed under the trees. One boy had a large grocery box which was tied on to his tricycle, and he rode about with this dragging behind him and a few thin sticks lying in the bottom.

Inside the house, children were in the lounge playing cards, listening to records, drawing or looking at books. One girl was knitting, another did a puzzle. A girl of fifteen, who was leaving at the end of the term, was being helped to write invitation cards for her leaving party. Some children were unwell with colds and had to stay in their bedrooms. During the day the houseparents kept an eye on them and tried to find time to spend with them, occasionally going in to read them a story or play cards.

In the recreation hall there was a group of three deaf children and three hearing children playing with large constructional wooden blocks and trucks. A housemother sat near them, mending Brownie uniforms. One very badly handicapped boy, aged ten, managed to push one of the wooden trucks through from the recreation hall, along the corridor, and into the lounge. It took him over twenty minutes and entailed going up a small slope; he had to crawl all the way. He was very hot and triumphant when he finally reached the lounge, and he received much praise from the staff for his efforts.

When Jimmy had finished breakfast the first thing he asked was, 'Take me to the playroom' (lounge). When he got there he found the curtains still drawn and the room in darkness. He said, 'Draw the curtains. They have a string, pull the string.' Then he asked to be taken out to the hall, where he got out of his wheelchair and talked to some visitors who were sitting on the settee, waiting to take out a child they had come to visit.

Then his housemother came to him and told him that she was going 'off' for a while. Jimmy said: 'No, no, don't go yet.' She sat down in the hall armchair and took him on her lap. He cuddled her and said again, 'Don't go off.' She sat in the armchair with him on her lap for a quarter of an hour and then said, 'Now, I really must go, I'll see you later.' She went away, first making sure that Jimmy, who appeared distressed, was handed over to another housemother who immediately suggested that he help her light the coal-fire in the lounge.

This was a thrilling job, and Jimmy eagerly hurried off with her. He helped the housemother to sweep and clean the grate and put the paper in the fire-place. All the while he kept on talking about the blackness of the coal and how he had helped to collect the wood during the previous afternoon. After the fire was lit Jimmy and the housemother sat back and watched the flames for a while. Then they put some more coal on, and fastened the guard round it. By that time other children were coming into the lounge and starting to play.

Jimmy said: 'We've got to fetch some more coal and some more wood now,' and the housemother agreed that the grate needed stacking up. For half an hour Jimmy helped the housemother fetch wood and coal from the end of a corridor which led into the garden and woodshed. The housemother went outside and broke up some wood, and Jimmy watched from the doorway. Then a box of wood was put on his wheel-chair and he held it steady as he was pushed back into the lounge, then he helped to tip the wood into a large old tin by the grate.

When Jimmy had had his hands washed he helped that same housemother to do the laundry; by that time it was nearly twelve o'clock. They put sheets and pillow cases into a small truck and wheeled it round the house, leaving clean laundry in each bedroom. In one bedroom two children were unwell and the housemother and Jimmy stopped to talk to them; they were sitting on the carpet playing with toys, and the school matron was helping them play. When the laundry truck was empty Jimmy was lifted inside for a ride, and wheeled away to get his hands washed and go to the lavatory.

At 12.15 p.m.: The first children started to go into the dining-room for lunch. Some of the very slow and badly handicapped children had started to be got ready, by having their hands washed and going to the lavatory, at just after 11.30. The more fidgety children, and those who found waiting particularly irksome, were left until last. One thirteen-year-old boy, engrossed in kicking a football, was allowed to continue playing until nearly 12.30. Some of the children had a fifteen-minute wait in the dining-room before lunch began.

12.30 p.m.: Lunch-time. Grace was said first, and lunch was fairly quiet because the children were hungry after being out of doors or playing energetically. Some of the older children helped to carry round the plates and, as usual, the children helped themselves to vegetables and potatoes from the dishes on their tables. Jimmy served the other children at his table, spilling a lot of the vegetables on purpose, and laughing and spilling cutlery on to the floor. He was the most excited child at his table.

Between 1.30 and 2.30 p.m.: The children had a rest, the younger ones lying down on their beds with the bedroom curtains drawn, and the older children sitting quietly in their bedrooms, talking, looking at books or following some quiet activity. Whilst the children rested, the housemothers did odd domestic jobs, tidied up, ironed some shirts and blouses on the landing outside the bedrooms, and did some sewing.

Between 2.30 and 4.45 p.m.: The children were free to play again, and as they went downstairs they decided on what they wanted to do. Some of the children built another blanket house in the lounge. One boy went outside on the terrace to draw; he was the very handicapped boy who had to draw with his foot, and he had a special drawing-board desk. Later on, when he was brought indoors, it was found that he had filled his drawing desk with weeds and earth which he had pulled up from between the terrace stones with his toes. He was laughing about this joke he had played on his houseparents.

Two pramloads of children went down the drive for a walk with two housemothers. There were four children in one pram, and five in another. They stopped the prams and watched the traffic at the end of the drive. Some children were taken to the back of the house, where they played on the swings and swingboats in the little playground. One housemother amused the children by doing acrobatics on a rail at the side. The children stayed in this playground for fifteen minutes.

By the front door, two nine-year-old boys got a bucket of water and 'cleaned' the car belonging to one of the houseparents. One of the cleaning boys could walk, the other was confined to a wheelchair. A housemother helped them with the car, and they threw lots of water on the car, and the boy in the wheel-chair held a dripping rag against the side of it.

In one of the upstairs bedrooms a girl with two visitors sorted out her clothes and talked about school.

Jimmy was one of the children who went for a walk in a pram. All the time on the walk the children who could speak chatted to each other and their housemothers.

'See all that mud.'

'Get that lump of wood, we need that.'

'Push us in that mud.'
'Look at that big ditch.'
'They put horses in that lorry, it's called a box.'
'There's the cake-shop.'
'Push the wheels in the mud.'

The pram walk took an hour and when Jimmy got back he decided that he wanted to stay outside, despite the chilliness of the weather, whilst the other children went indoors. From a quarter to four until half past four he rode up and down alone along the garden paths. At one point he got off his tricycle and played garages for a long time, crouching down in a rose-bed and pretending to fill the tricycle with petrol. Earth was his make-believe petrol, and Jimmy poured handfuls of it all over the back of the tricycle. When he was called in to be got ready for supper he was covered in earth, with mud down his rubber boots and in his clothes. He was so outstandingly grubby that the staff had to laugh. He was taken to the toilet to be cleaned up. Then he went into the lounge and played for about ten minutes, romping and fighting on the mattress on the floor, and thumping himself into the laps of the housemothers who were sitting on the floor or in armchairs.

At 5 p.m.: Everybody was ready for tea. It had been decided to have a 'picnic' tea in the lounge. This was because some lucky children had gone home for the week-end, and the staff wanted to make a little change for the children who had been left behind, or who, like Jimmy, had little contact with their families. Some children sat on the mattress on the floor, and others sat in the armchairs which had been arranged in a circle around the mattress, others were in wheel-chairs in the circle. They had sandwiches, tomatoes, jelly, trifle, biscuits, sweets and tea. As they ate they watched some skating on the television. The more able children helped the very handicapped ones, unwrapping their sweets for them and putting chocolates into their mouths, holding their drinks up to their mouths for them, or even feeding them their jelly and trifle. A lot of trifle got spilt in one armchair, and two cups of tea were tipped over on the mattress, but this was soon mopped up.

At 5.50 p.m.: The television was switched off and the children started to go up to their bedrooms to get ready for bed. Some had baths, others washed at the hand-basins in their bedrooms. In the youngest children's bedroom two little girls had their hair washed and it was dried for them as they sat in a corner of the bedroom. As the children got into their nightdresses or pyjamas and dressing-gowns they played with toys, either on their beds or on the floor. One or two of the children helped their housemothers to dust the shoes on a piece of newspaper on the bedroom floor.

Jimmy was going to have a bath, and before his housemother was ready to take him he played on the floor in the bedroom, crawling about and teasing other children about who was to have a bath that evening. He opened the wardrobe door, and pretended to read the bath-list which was pinned inside, saying solemnly, 'Miss . . . and Miss . . . for a bath tonight,' and causing much laughter among the other children. Somehow, amidst all this romping about, the children managed to get themselves ready for bed, some beginning to wash at the basins, and others undressing themselves as much as they could. Peter lay on the floor, laughing at Jimmy's antics.

At 6 p.m.: Jimmy was taken to be bathed by his housemother.

At 6.20 p.m.: He came back into the bedroom. He was allowed to help dry the hair of the little girls who had been sitting in the corner with another housemother drying their hair with the hand-dryer. Jimmy was allowed to turn the dryer on and off carefully two or three times.

Between 6.30 and 7 p.m.: Most of the children in Jimmy's bedroom were sitting on, or in, their beds, and playing with toys. They had wooden bricks, cars, a musical box, dolls, plastic interlocking bricks, a plastic garage and a puzzle. There was a continual exchange of toys from child to child. Sometimes the housemother handed the toys over to different children, sometimes the children reached them across themselves. During this period the housemother stayed in the bedroom with the children, sorting out some laundry. Also, matron came round with some medicines.

At 7.20 p.m.: The children were fairly settled, and had had their toys put away and the lights turned off. The toys were put on their lockers, on the window-sills or into the wardrobe. Then the children were given 'good-night' cuddles, tucked up and left.

The older children, twelve and over, went downstairs in their dressing-gowns and watched television for a little while. Just before going to bed, these older children were given some fruit to eat, and another drink.

Impressions of Fieldway

The overall impression of Fieldway was that it was a temporary *home* for the children. There was a relaxed air and the children were not harassed; their daily routines were not bound by organizational regulations. One example of this was that they washed as any child at home might, in a small basin in the bedroom or bathroom, with a minimum delay and no queueing. Even the most handicapped children were given the chance to spend time dangling their hands in wash-basins, trying to turn taps on and looking at themselves in wall mirrors above the basins; their toothbrushes were kept in individual holders and they possessed their own toothpaste. Their bathing was done by their own houseparents and never took place on a 'rota system' in which one adult undresses a child, then hands him over to another adult to bath and a third adult to dry and dress. The bathroom accommodation was very attractive, also, being very spacious and with ample privacy, curtains, partitions and imaginative wall tiles.

The children had opportunities for developing independence, being encouraged to dress on their own as much as possible; even the severely handicapped children were allowed to try and wriggle their way out of shirts and blouses. They folded their own clothes if they could, and straightened their beds, and the older children had a lot of responsibility in keeping their own bedrooms clean and tidy. Being independent meant that household chores took longer, but the staff agreed that such experiences were essential for the children. Mealtime independence was particularly noticeable, with even the youngest children helping each other to vegetables, and pouring tea, whilst the older children took turns at laying tables and tidying up the dining-room. Fieldway meal routines were of a high standard, with the dining-room always attractively arranged and peaceful. Conversation was encouraged, and consideration was given to others: the children did not leave the table until everyone had finished at that table, and offered other people food before helping themselves. Considering the severe multiple handicaps of the children, and their mental limitation, and the fact that some of them had behaviour problems, it was not easy to achieve a good standard of mealtime behaviour, but the staff made a definite and successful attempt to do so. The fact that the staff sat down at the tables, beside the children they had to feed, added to the stability of the room.

Another very impressive feature of Fieldway School was the way the staff participated in the children's activities; for example, organizing ball games in the garden, and 'pass the parcel' and 'musical hats' games in the lounge. The staff also made attempts to see that the children had opportunity for individual adult company if possible; for example, a houseparent sometimes did her sewing near a child who was doing a puzzle on his own, and so gave the child a chance of attention and chat; and, as with Jimmy, they sometimes let the children help with household chores and thus get adult attention. There was very good communication between the staff and the children, which was noticeable most of all at bedtime, when the houseparents would chat to their bedroom groups in much the same way as a real mother would.

The children were very fond of the staff and sometimes they became quite distressed when a houseparent went off duty. This was understandable; any child in a close-knit family would react in the same way if the mother suddenly decided to take herself off on her own for the day. Although the children's reactions were normal and showed evidence of the strong bond between them and their houseparents, they nevertheless made one realize that, although a residential school can do everything in its power to make a homely environment for the children, it still remains a substitute for a real home because real parents never go 'off duty'. This is an acceptable aspect of residential schools, since their function is not generally to *replace* the home; when children have a happy understanding home and family one would not wish the school to usurp the function of the parents; but, for the deprived child, like Jimmy, suffering a certain amount of family rejection, the school becomes more than a temporary term-time home and he suffers an extra deprivation when his houseparent goes off duty, or leaves the school. Fieldway staff tried to combat this problem by making sure that those particularly deprived children had another special houseparent who would take an interest in them; hence Jimmy's housemother handed him over to the other houseparent who immediately enlisted his help with making the fire.

Another outstanding feature of Fieldway was that the children were not frantically possessive about their toys. Although there were occasional quarrels and plenty of teasing, there was remarkably little toy-snatching and destruction. This may have been because there was ample space in the house, there was always some safe place in which to put a toy – on a window-sill, behind the settee, down the edge of a chair, or on the beds – and the children were not 'on top' of each other all the time. The mixing of age groups also had a steadying effect on the younger, more tempestuous children, and the adolescent children were often seen reprimanding the younger ones and showing them what to do.

Generally, Fieldway School gave a very favourable impression of child care and home-making. The children, being multiply handicapped and all with some degree of mental retardation, represented one of the most seriously disabled groups of children I have ever seen all living under one roof; this might easily have provided an excuse for institutionalizing the organization, but in fact this had not been allowed to happen.

2. Ridge Hospital

Ridge Hospital was in a country area, very poorly served by public transport, away from the main road, and several miles from a town or village. The hospital consisted of various buildings spread over a wide area of open heathland. It was under the administration of a Regional Hospital Board, and specialized in taking children who had severe chronic handicaps; most of the children were in need of long-term residential care. There was a school attached to the hospital, employing qualified teachers under the administration of the Local Authority.

The ward observed at Ridge accommodated eighteen children aged from six to ten. Ten were handicapped by spina bifida, one by cerebral palsy and deafness, the rest were handicapped by the effects of congenital bone disorders or thalidomide. Their intelligence varied from above average down to educational subnormality. Most of the children needed some help with dressing and toileting, but the deaf cerebral palsied boy was the only one to need feeding aid. Three of the children were in need of real nursing care, because of their complicated physical disorders. One child was in plaster, and required temporary hospital care.

The ward was part of a building put up in the 1930s, and was on a first floor. There were eighteen beds and cots, in two long rows down the long ward. Leading from the ward was the sister's office, a small 'hobbies' room, and swing-doors at each end which led on to small landings. A narrow walled balcony also led from the ward.

One landing had the kitchen, domestic and spare rooms on it, plus a lift. The children were not allowed on to this landing as the stairs were not gated. The kitchen was used for preparing cold food only, e.g. cornflakes, bread and butter, drinks, etc.; no real cooking took place there. The domestic and spare rooms were used for storing brooms or sweepers, and for staff changing rooms. The landing at the other end of the ward led to the bathroom and toilets. Children were allowed on this landing, on their way to the bathroom, as the stairs here were gated.

In the bathroom there was room for three small hand-basins, one bath, a wooden toilet chair and a wooden table. Yellow plastic chamber pots were on the floor. In another small room on this landing was a table and small cupboards; this room was used for any special treatments that might need to take place, such as dressings.

There were only two toilets for the ward, and these had to serve eighteen children. They were situated in the bathroom, partitioned and with doors. Because the bathroom and toilet accommodation was so cramped, some of the children were given bed-pans or bottles to use in the ward. No screens were available, and some children were given urine bottles standing openly in the middle of the ward. The other children took no notice of this common practice.

Some children also had blanket baths on their beds, again because of the cramped conditions in the bathroom. One nurse described this procedure as 'for convenience's sake'.

There were no mirrors above the hand-basins in the bathroom; toothbrushes and tooth-mugs were kept all together on a tray on the bathroom table. Over the portable toilet chair (a type of commode) in the corner of the bathroom there were rows of wooden hooks on which were hung towels and flannels. Immediately above these hooks was a narrow shelf holding hair-brushes and combs.

The tooth-mugs, the brushes and the combs had numbers on them, as well as the children's names; these names and numbers were written on pink sticky plaster and stuck on. The toothbrushes had only numbers written on them which the children had to remember.

Hair-washing took place in the bathroom, usually first thing on a Saturday morning, when nearly all eighteen children might be finished by 9.30. Their hair was dried in the ward with a hand hair-dryer.

Week-day school was held in the ward for one half of the children, and in the hobbies room for the rest. At the week-end the children were allowed access to the hobbies room. But most of the time was spent in the ward, where they ate, slept and played. Certain 'reliable' children were sometimes allowed, singly, into the kitchen, to watch tea or drinks being prepared by the orderly. They were sometimes allowed to go into sister's office, if sister or a senior nurse was there. The children were all allowed to use the balcony when the weather was dry. It was rather difficult to see over the wall of the balcony as it was high, but they could just see over if in their wheel-chairs or on their beds. They never used the hospital grounds unless a visitor or the nurses wheeled them out as a special treat.

The walls of the ward were painted grey, and there was grey mottled lino on the floor. There were no carpets, armchairs, settees, curtains or wallpaper. There were four small Victorian children's pictures placed high on the walls of the ward; and at one end there was a high piece of peg-board on which a school picture from a magazine had been pegged. The beds and cots were hospital-type, high, and difficult for children to get down from unaided. However, on my second visit to this ward, six months later, two divan-type beds had been acquired for two children who had been handicapped by thalidomide, as an aid to their independence, and they had been taught to roll off these beds almost unaided.

Beside each bed was a very battered grey metal locker, the doors and drawers of which were difficult to open because they stuck badly. The children kept their belongings and some clothes in these lockers. Clean clothes were kept in the bathroom linen cupboard. There were no wardrobes, dressing-tables or mirrors in the ward, although dressing-tables and wardrobes were stored in the spare room beside the kitchen on the landing.

There was a piano in the ward, and a television set at one end, on a high table, beneath which was a record-player and radio on a shelf. Chairs and tables for use at mealtimes and school were stacked high in one corner of the ward and in the little hobbies room. The hobbies room was small and mostly walled in glass; it had low sliding cupboards and good working-tops above the cupboards. There were two fish-tanks in this room, and a toy fort. Children's books were in the cupboards.

Meals were sent from a central hospital kitchen and served from a meal trolley plugged into the wall. The children did not see the food cooked and were not aware of such processes as peeling potatoes and making pastry. All meals were eaten in the ward. Some of the children sat in their wheel-chairs and had their food on plates on their laps, others sat at small tables which had been pushed together. Others stayed in bed or cots.

On one occasion I saw six children eating at one small table, five in wheel-chairs which the nurses had arranged in two rows one behind the other, one having his meal in bed on the balcony, and the cerebral palsied deaf boy sitting well apart from the other children; he was the only child in the ward who required feeding and he was usually fed apart from the others, with the nurse standing in front of him. On another occasion the children were all jostling around throughout the whole meal, and one boy ate his meal leaning sideways out of his wheel-chair, eating his food from his plate underneath the television table on a shelf piled with old magazines and books.

There was often a lot of moving around during meal-times, with children pushing their wheel-chairs up and down the ward while they waited for their second course. The senior nurse on duty usually stood at the trolley to serve the meal, and the other nurses walked to and fro handing the plates to the children. The children did not wait for each other to begin eating; and during meals the staff constantly reminded the children to be quiet, to hurry and to eat quickly. The children often shouted and argued with each other as they waited for their second course, not heeding their nurses' pleas to be quiet.

The tables were not laid with mats, serving-spoons, side-plates or second-course utensils. When a child received his sweet course he would have his spoon put in the bowl for him at the same time. Vegetable dishes were never put on the tables, although most of the children were mentally and physically capable of serving themselves and each other; the vegetables were served from the metal containers on the trolley.

Plates of bread and butter or cakes were not put out to be

chosen as required, but put on to the children's plates by the nurses; nor did they ever pour their own drinks. The children never took part in helping to serve the meal or stack plates or tidy up afterwards. And they did not wait until all had finished before they began moving about, going to the toilet or getting undressed or bathed.

The children never saw adults eating because the nurses always had their meals in a separate canteen block away from the wards.

Breakfast routines were split between night-staff and day-staff, the first part of breakfast (cereals, drinks, bread and butter) being served by night-staff, and prepared in the ward kitchen. It was wheeled into the ward on a trolley, covered by a cloth, as the children began to get up in the morning. The second part of breakfast (cooked in the central kitchen and sent in containers: eggs, bacon, sausage, etc.) was served by the day-staff as they came on duty. The hot part of breakfast was sometimes served between fifteen and thirty minutes after the cold part.

Staff

The staff consisted of two sisters and a staff nurse, and trainee or auxiliary nurses. There were sometimes five trainees attached to one ward, but as duty times varied they would not always be 'on' at the same time. It was usual for the sister and staff nurses to remain for some months, or even years, on one ward, but trainees changed every three months to another ward. Not all the trainees would be changed at the same time, so it was customary for there to be two or three nurses in the ward who had been there for several weeks, plus two or three who were very new. The ages of the trainees were from sixteen to eighteen, and they usually worked in Ridge Hospital prior to going on to general or children's nursing training in other hospitals. Sometimes they were filling in time before going to train as nursery nurses or teachers, or before going up to University. Some of the youngest trainees were gaining hospital experience before making up their minds whether to take up nursing or not. The older auxiliary nurses were sometimes qualified nurses from overseas, who were in England for a few months or a year to learn the language and get English hospital experience. Other auxiliary nurses were qualified nursery nurses who were gaining hospital experience. Some were middle-aged unqualified married women who lived out and worked part-time.

Day-staff worked from 7.30 a.m. until 8.30 p.m., with various hours off during the day; they either did a late evening with time off during the afternoon or they did a long stretch on duty and finished in the afternoon. If they were going to work during the late evening (up to 8.30 p.m.) they had 3½ hours off during the afternoon. All nurses had two clear days off each week.

Night-staff worked from 7.30 p.m. until 8.30 a.m. They were usually changed every three months, although it was not unknown for older night-nurses, who liked night-duty and found it convenient, to remain for longer. Night-staff duties included preparing the cold breakfast trolley, getting the children out of bed and partly dressing them in the morning, toileting as necessary during the night and in the morning, tidying the beds, and looking after any children who were ill in the night.

When day-staff arrived in the ward they had to read the duty list, which informed them which children they would 'do' that day, and their ward duties. The sister decided which nurses should see to different children, and the list varied each day in order to give the nurse experience in handling different types of handicap and different children. The nurses' duties actually connected with handling the children included washing them, dressing, bathing, toileting, giving out meals and drinks. Their duties connected with the domestic organization of the ward consisted of tidying lockers, sweeping floors, washing chamber pots, preparing bread and butter, turning down, airing and straightening beds, wiping lockers, sorting out clothes, polishing the piano, preparing drinks, wiping chairs and tables, and tidying up the bathroom, the ward, the hobbies room and the sluice-room.

Visitors

Personal visitors were permitted, but in one week-end I saw only three children with visitors. The children were permitted one week-end in four at home (if treatment allowed this). But many of the children were rejected, so did not get visitors or home trips. Voluntary helpers from the Hospital League of Friends brought a hospital shop-trolley around the wards every Sunday afternoon; they knew the children and chatted to them.

There were no facilities for visitors and all visiting took place in the ward or day-room with the other children.

Diary of a Week-end

A Saturday for Christopher

Christopher was aged nine, and badly handicapped by athetoid cerebral palsy and deafness. He could be described as totally dependent because he needed feeding, he could not walk or hold anything, and he required help with toileting. He had no speech. (However, he was physically stronger than Peter of Fieldway School, as his head control was good, whereas Peter's head control was very poor and his limbs were much 'floppier' than Christopher's.) Christopher's achievements were limited by his physical disabilities, but his alert facial expression and the interest he showed when watching other children suggested that he was not mentally backward. He had been in Ridge Hospital since he was five years old, most of the time in the same ward.

At 7.30 a.m. on a bright early spring Saturday, Christopher was sitting in his wheel-chair and a day-nurse was feeding him his hot breakfast; the nurse stood in front of him, holding the plate in one hand and the spoon in the other, quite high up. Christopher could not see what was on the plate. He had earlier been fed his cereals, by a night-nurse. He was dressed in a shirt and pullover and his pyjama trousers. He finished his breakfast at a quarter to eight, and then until 8.30 he sat and waited for a nurse to take him to the bathroom. He did not have anything on his wheel-chair table-tray, although at one point another child gave him a broken wind-up toy and he smiled; the toy fell to the floor as he put his hand on it, and a nurse picked it up as she passed down the ward and put it back on his tray; but five minutes later it fell down again and then remained on the floor.

At 8.30 *a.m.*: Christopher was wheeled into the bathroom and lifted on to the wooden 'potty-chair' (the commode) which was in the corner of the room, underneath the row of hooks which held towels and flannels. Other children were being bathed or washed, or were going to the lavatory on little yellow plastic chamber pots on the floor all around Christopher. Christopher sat in the potty-chair until 9 o'clock. Nobody spoke to him.

At 9 a.m.: Christopher was wheeled back into the ward and put on his cot, where he had his trousers put on, and his shoes and socks. Then he was lifted into his wheel-chair and taken back to the bathroom, this time to have his face washed. He went back to the ward at 9.30 and was pushed into the little hobbies room for ten minutes as the ward floor was being swept.

From 9.40 until 12.5: Christopher sat in his wheel-chair by the piano at one end of the ward. He had nothing on his chair-tray. He was given a drink just before 11 o'clock. Then, for a few minutes after drinks another child went up to him and 'wrestled' with him; this made him laugh and he waved his arms and got very excited. This same child then fetched him three torn playing cards, put them on his tray for a few minutes and then ran off with them again. Christopher spent two hours and twenty-five minutes in this same spot by the piano, and during that time none of the ward staff spoke to him or put anything on his tray.

From 12.5 until 12.30 p.m.: Christopher was being fed his lunch, still sitting by the piano and slightly apart from other children who were eating. The nurse did not sign to him or speak to him as she fed him. After he had been fed he remained still sitting in the same place until 1 o'clock.

At 1 p.m.: Christopher was taken to the bathroom, toileted on the 'potty-chair', then washed and put into his pyjamas.

At 1.30 p.m.: Christopher, now in pyjamas and dressing-gown, was pushed back into the ward and placed near the piano again.

From 1.30 until 4.15 p.m.: Christopher sat in the same place, by the piano. He had nothing to do, and was not moved about the ward at all. Nobody spoke to him or signed to him. During this 2¾-hour period of sitting in one place with nothing to do, three children made a procession with their wheel-chairs one behind the other and 'marched' down the ward between the beds. Christopher, who all the time watched the children intently, laughed at the procession and waved his arms with pleasure. The nurses tidied up the ward, polished the lockers and the piano and turned down the beds. At 4 o'clock the television was switched on and the children stared solemnly at wrestling and boxing. Christopher was not moved into a position to watch.

At 4.15 p.m.: It was supper time. Christopher was fed by a nurse who stood in front of him with the plate held up high; he could not see what was on the plate. Some of the other children ate their suppers as they watched television sporting programmes, holding their plates on their laps. During suppertime there was a change of staff and another group of nurses took over the serving. No nurse was seen to speak to Christopher at any time during supper.

At 5 p.m.: Christopher was taken to the toilet, then washed.

By 5.25 p.m.: He was lying in his cot.

From 5.25 until 7 p.m.: Christopher was lying flat in his cot, watching the other children. Nobody gave him anything to do, nor communicated with him in any way.

At 7 p.m.: Lights were put out, after the children had been given a last drink.

*

When I first met Christopher, six months earlier on a bright autumn Sunday, I then observed that he spent long empty hours with nothing to do. That particular Sunday afternoon he had sat in a corner of the balcony for 2½ hours, unable to see over the wall, with nothing on his tray to look at, and also in a position a little apart from the other children so that he could not comfortably watch them. That afternoon he was fed his supper by one nurse, and whilst she was feeding him another nurse came along. The first nurse remarked: 'Oh, you can feed him if you've got nothing else to do, I don't want to do him.' So, the second nurse took over Christopher's feeding, standing in front of him, again with the plate held high, and talking across him to another nurse as she spooned his food into his mouth.

A Sunday for Tony

Tony was aged eight and handicapped by spina bifida. He could not walk because he had lost the use of his lower limbs. He had good hands and could feed himself, and was able to propel himself around competently in his wheel-chair. He needed some assistance in getting to the lavatory and being bathed. He appeared to have some mental limitation, although this was not to a serious degree. He had been in Ridge Hospital for just over two years.

It was 6 a.m. on a dark, cold, early spring morning. A group of six children were sitting round a table, looking at scrapbooks and old *Bumper Annuals*. There were thirteen children in the ward that morning, as some children had gone away for the week-end. Four children had to stay in bed to be attended to by the day-staff, so the two night-nurses had to get nine children out of bed. They did not have to wash the children, do their hair, nor toilet them unless absolutely necessary, nor did they have to dress them fully; but by 6 o'clock the nine children were waiting for breakfast (which would be served at 7.15).

Tony was sitting in his wheel-chair, dressed in shirt, jumper, nappie and slippers; he did not have any trousers on. He wheeled himself up and down the ward with another child in a wheelchair. At my appearance in the ward the children all set up a clamour of, 'Lady, lady, come here, come here and talk to us.' The four children still in bed asked to be given things from out of their lockers.

From 6 until 7.15 a.m.: Tony alternately pushed himself up and down the ward between the beds and cots, or just sat still. The night-nurses busied themselves with the beds and tidying up the ward. They put the Light Programme on very loudly at 7 o'clock.

At 7.15 a.m.: The two night-nurses brought the trolley into the ward and served the cold part of breakfast: bread and butter and cereals. Tony rested his cereal bowl on his bare thighs, his nappie showing below his jumper.

At 7.30 a.m.: The day-staff came on duty, at the same time as the hot part of breakfast arrived from the central kitchen. The night-nurses stopped serving breakfast and moved away to finish the beds, and the day staff took over the breakfast, but none of the

Children in Hospitals 85

children seemed very interested in the sausages and scrambled eggs as they had already filled up with cereals and bread and butter. As breakfast was being served the children in wheelchairs constantly moved around between the table, the beds and each other's wheel-chairs.

Just before 8 o'clock Tony pushed himself into the sister's little office, and he stayed there for a few moments and watched the nurses reading the day's duty lists. There were four day-staff then on duty, plus one night-nurse who was still doing beds. Tony was still wearing his night nappy-square, and did not have any trousers on.

At 8.5 a.m.: Tony was put on to a bed-pan on his bed. The pan was standing on a rubber sheet. He sat there, not saying anything, there was no screen round him. The day staff were all busy getting the children toileted, washed or bathed, and fully dressed.

At 8.45 a.m.: Tony was lifted off the bed-pan. He had sat there for forty minutes.

From 8.45 until 9.15 a.m.: Tony first sat on his bed whilst he was helped to dress, then he was wheeled into the bathroom to have his face washed. The senior nurse on duty was extremely patient with him as she encouraged him to do his own buttons up on his shirt-sleeves (this was the only training in independence and dressing that was observed during the whole week-end in that ward).

At 9 o'clock the Light Programme was turned off, having been on very loudly for two hours with the children shouting and arguing above the noise of it.

From 9.15 until 10.5 a.m.: Tony either sat at the end of the ward staring into the sister's office, or propelled himself up and down the ward between the beds. Then, at five past ten, the nurses arranged the children in a circle at one end of the ward. Ten children were up, either in wheel-chairs or on ordinary chairs, and three were lying dressed on their beds. They had to wait in the circle for the arrival of the hospital chaplain, who would take the Sunday School Service. While the children waited for the chaplain, the nurses tidied up the other end of the ward; they swept the floor, tidied some linen and clothes and pushed some of the beds out on to the balcony to air. Outside, the early spring sunshine had cleared the frost from the lawns and the sky was a thin cloudless blue.

At 10.30 a.m.: The chaplain arrived in a rush, with cries of, 'Hello, children, hello there!' The children had silently sat waiting for him for twenty minutes, so they greeted him with some excitement and relief. Sunday School lasted fifteen minutes. The chaplain talked about pancakes, then he played the piano and the children sang 'All things bright and beautiful' and 'Glad that I live am I'. When the service finished the chaplain departed through the swing-doors at the other end of the ward, with a cheery wave of his hand, and the children dispersed from their circle and roamed up and down the ward.

Between 10.45 and 11.45 a.m.: Tony wandered out on to the balcony, which was crammed with beds being aired in the sun. There was not much room and it was difficult for him to see over the wall, but he pushed his way up and down as there was just room for his wheel-chair to pass between the empty beds and the balcony wall. The nurses continued to tidy up the ward. Tony pushed in from the balcony and announced: 'It would be nice to go out.' There was no answer from anyone. He said again, a little louder: 'I wish we could go for a walk.' One or two other children set up cries of: 'Are we going out, oh, will sister let us go out?' The nurses did not answer.

Some children kept looking unsuccessfully for paper and pencils, trying to open their stiff metal lockers. Several children squabbled about pencils and snatched them from each other. The three children who had to stay in bed had some pencils and they kept them carefully hidden under their pillows so that the mobile children could not grab them as they went by in their wheel-chairs. The nurses continued to tidy up.

Some of the children sat and quietly watched the nurses working. One backward boy asked for a broom and, after he had pleaded incessantly for some time, the nurses let him sweep the floor at one end of the ward.

The children had drinks, and some of them had their hair washed.

Tony still milled round the beds on the balcony. At one point he found a toy policeman's hat and put it on his head.

Children in Hospitals 87

At 11.45 a.m.: The children were arranged for lunch. Some were in their wheel-chairs, and some sat round the table. Three children were in bed.

Between 11.55 and 12.35: Lunch was being eaten. Tony sat in his wheel-chair, with his plate balanced on his lap. He did not help himself to vegetables, as they were served from the trolley containers. His cutlery was given to him at the same time as his plate of food.

From 12.35 p.m. onwards: After lunch finished Tony pushed himself slowly up and down the ward, not saying anything. Once he went into the hobbies room, where it was very cold as no sun shone on that side. Two other children were in there, and Tony looked at a book for five minutes. The other children went back into the ward and Tony followed them, with a pen he had found in the hobbies room. The pen belonged to another child and there was a heated argument about its possession. Tony accidentally snapped the pen in two, and there was some distressed crying from the child to whom it had belonged. The nurses brought in the beds from the balcony, arranged them in straight rows and turned down the covers neatly, ready for bedtime; it was then about 1.30. Next, the nurses tidied up the tops of the lockers again and dusted the piano.

Tony again just pushed himself up and down the ward, or sat still. Some of the children asked me to find pencils and paper for them, but there were none available anywhere. Tony called over to me: 'Shall we talk, can we talk?'

One little girl played with a doll's pram, completely absorbed in putting dolls in and out (this was the only example of play during the whole day in that ward).

At 2.15 p.m.: A visitor came to a child. Tony sat a little way off and stared solemnly at the visitor, who sat by the television set and had tea and biscuits as she talked to her little girl. Tony, sitting and staring at the visitor, was joined by other children in wheel-chairs who gradually gathered round. These children formed a small circle a short distance away from the visitor and her child and silently watched them. The scene resembled shy animals encircling a strange sight and it was as embarrassing for the visitor as it was pathetic for the children who stared. Tony and the circle of children watched the visitor continuously until 2.45.

After 2.15 the children were all kept out of the hobbies room as the sister was expecting an important visitor and wanted to take her into that room, and she did not want a book or chair to be out of place. She cleared the benches of books, and the interlocking chairs were stacked one on top of the other. Sister kept going nervously back into the room, putting a chair to one side, or re-arranging a book, and finally she shut the door firmly and said: 'No children are to go in there again this afternoon.' The children did not seem to mind. The hobbies room, with its toy fort, and cupboards full of rather old-fashioned books, was made very little use of anyway.

One of the children was got ready for bed and in pyjamas at 2.40. Then, at 2.45 the hospital shop-trolley arrived. Pocket money was in the children's individual purses, which were all kept together in a large old biscuit tin in sister's office. Just before the shop arrived the sister fetched the tin and handed round the purses. The woman who brought the shop-trolley round the hospital was a former sister, and the children still called her 'sister' although she was no longer wearing uniform. Two other voluntary workers helped her with the shop. The children enjoyed choosing their purchases, and they bought sweets, balloons, toy divers, a ball, a rubber, ear-rings and pencils. Tony bought himself a ball, and a card to send to his mother; the card had been suggested and chosen for him by one of the voluntary women.

When the shop went away the sister collected up the purses again and put them away in the tin. The children sat and looked at what they had bought.

From 3.30 p.m. onwards: The television was switched on and Tony and another child sat and watched the visitor, whilst other children moved around, sometimes watching television. The nurses continued to clean lockers and then sorted out jumpers, socks and other clothes.

Tony continued to watch the visitor until ten past four, sitting quite still in one spot. He did not take any notice of the television. Then, at 4.15 he had his tea, holding his plate on his knees and sitting close to the television screen and watching a film.

At 4.30 p.m.: Most of the children were being got ready for bed, either being in the bathroom, having washes or going to the toilet, or being undressed in the ward. But at 5 o'clock Tony was still picking at his tea, holding the plate on his lap at the same time as moving up and down the ward or watching television.

Between 5 and 6.45 p.m.: Tony wandered up and down the ward, whilst he waited his turn to be got ready for bed. He finished his tea, moved away from the television set and looked for something to do. He found a pair of toy false teeth and put them in his mouth, then hurried down the ward in his chair, roaring with laughter and showing all the other children his funny mouth. He played with the teeth for five minutes, then found a piece of torn yellow balloon. He put this in his mouth and chewed it. The teeth were claimed angrily by another child.

Tony watched television again for a little while, then again propelled himself round the ward. At 6 o'clock the television was switched off and the radio Light Programme was put on very loudly.

Many of the children were then in bed, whilst others were still being undressed or washed. There was a lot of squabbling and crying and shouting above the noise of very loud pop music from the radio.

At 6.45 p.m.: Tony was taken to be got ready for bed; he was the last child to be put to bed and was quite quickly undressed, toileted and washed.

At 7 p.m.: The lights were put out after the children had been given a last drink, and a quick 'good-night' cuddle from the senior nurse.

*

After the lights were put out, Tony's card for his mother was found trampled and torn on the floor, where he must have dropped it unheeded during one of his wanderings between the beds.

Elsewhere in Ridge Hospital, a ground-floor ward accommodated twenty-four mentally able children, aged from four to six, who were physically handicapped by spina bifida or thalidomide. Although this ward had a day-room and access to a small paved courtyard, life there was as restricted as in the upstairs ward.

As in the other ward, the children's personal belongings were numbered. One day I asked an orderly why they did not just write the names of the children on their brushes and combs and toothbrushes, and she replied: 'Well, you could not do that, because they've always been given numbers. When a new child comes he takes over a vacant number, you see.'

'But wouldn't it be much easier for *you* to just remember the child's name rather than have to remember his name *and* a number?'

'No, because they *always* have ward numbers,' the orderly patiently repeated to me. Suddenly turning to a four-year-old child with spina bifida, the orderly then demanded: 'Here, what's your number?' He looked at her blankly. 'And what are your numbers, eh?' she turned to three other children, who answered with some hesitation and mistakes. She then busied herself at the toothbrush shelf before calling out 'Number –' and handing one of the thalidomide-handicapped children a toothbrush onto which had been squeezed a tiny length of paste from the communal tube.

The lavatory and bathroom accommodation on this ward was inadequate, and it was not unusual for naked and half-naked limbless four-year-olds to sit on their little yellow plastic pots, tight together, in a row against the bare wall, for an hour or an hour and a half, whilst bathing routines went on above and around them.

The going-to-bed routine for these little children started at 3.30 when they were lifted from the tables as they finished their tea and put on a sheet which lay in a corner of the room. Here they were stripped by one member of staff, who piled their discarded clothes into a heap on the floor and then handed the children to other members of staff who took them into the bathroom for potting and bathing. Children who were still finishing their tea could see children in the bathroom because the bathroom and day-room were opposite. When children were finished in the bathroom they were put into night-clothes, returned to the day-room and placed in front of the television until 6 o'clock while various sporting programmes, football results and films persisted noisily and meaninglessly above them.

Because these small mentally alert children had no opportunities to satisfy their normal craving for play, they inevitably derived bizarre play habits from their institutional environment. For example, even the badly handicapped thalidomide children were very adroit at wriggling along when on their pots, and, if left unsupervised, they would hide themselves, still attached to pots, in corners of the bathroom or behind the doors. On one occasion, seven thalidomide children on pots manoeuvred themselves into the cubicle lavatory, and, despite the energetic kicks of an armless boy who was sitting on the lavatory, they all managed to get into the cubicle. After a great effort they triumphantly closed the cubicle door, although to do this meant that the first ones in had to wriggle themselves and their pots almost behind the lavatory on to the waste pipe.

On another occasion they amused themselves by playing with the mess of food and plates which had been left over from lunchtime. The floor and tables were littered with dirty plates and spilt food, so the children went around collecting the plates and licking them clean of any remains of gravy, ice-cream and pudding. Then one little boy found a tiny watering-can and he filled this with apple purée which he scraped from the bottom of used pudding bowls. When the little can was full he carefully poured out small portions to the other children, who circled him and held out sticky plates and spoons. The little group solemnly ate the purée as they stood round the watering-can, which they had placed on the floor. Then another child went to the food trolley, gathered pieces of meat and pudding from the scraps bowl, took them back to the group, and shared them out with scrupulous fairness. Going back to the trolley and concentrating on the conglomeration in the scraps bowl, trying to make up his mind which pieces of pudding or meat he wanted next, he was surprised to have his trousers suddenly pulled down by a passing nurse as she hurried into the room to collect the children. She told him: 'Undress now, go to the bathroom, quick, we are late.' The nurse fetched the other children and picked up the plates and the can, ignoring the odd play scene which she had interrupted and not appearing to notice anything unusual in it.

The staff made little attempt to interest the children, nor did they communicate *consistently* with them. One morning, a young nurse passed a child who was haphazardly turning the pages of a scrap-book and she briskly said: 'Find the picture of the bears for me.'

He hunted eagerly for the little picture of 'The three bears' but when he looked up the nurse had gone, and she did not mention the bears next time she passed, although he held up the book and called out to her; so, with abject movements he pushed the book away.

There were very few *whole* toys or books for the children. During the rest-period after lunch, one little four-year-old, handicapped by thalidomide, asked me to open his locker for him and all it contained was one very torn and grubby *Rupert Annual* which he cradled against his chest as he went to sleep. The four-year-old girl in the next cot had only half-a-dozen picture postcards in her locker, which had been sellotaped to the inside of the locker door.

The long, dull periods that these children spent waiting for routine procedures caused hand-flapping and rocking habits. One five-year-old armless boy was seen to rock rhythmically backwards and forwards, non-stop for twenty minutes, unheeded by the staff who were near him. It was common for the children to sit unoccupied at bare tables in the day-room from before 6 until 7.30 a.m., some half-dressed, some still in their nightwear, quarrelling, crying, rocking, staring, waiting for the day-staff to arrive and serve hot breakfast. On dark winter mornings, with no sign of life in the grounds and the electric lights shining blankly on to the large dark uncurtained windows, the reflected scene was one of garish discomfort as these bored, active, thwarted children, some limbless, others partially paralysed, demonstrated their distress to an unresponding environment.

Impressions of Ridge

The most striking impression was how restricted the children were; they lived under such cramped conditions that there was never a chance to be alone, and there was no privacy even when going to the lavatory. Life went on round the beds with sleeping, playing, eating, washing, treatments, visitors, and sometimes even toileting, going on at the same time in the one room. A child such as Tony, who was not ill but was an in-patient because he needed schooling, physiotherapy and a home, had to sit on a bed-pan in his bed just as if he was a sick patient recovering from an operation; this was simply because there was no room in the bathroom and it was quicker to put him on a bed-pan. Because the ward was upstairs there was no access to the outside, and even on the brightest of days the children remained indoors. This was particularly shocking when one realized that the children did not live in the ward for just a few weeks, but that it was their home for several years.

There was a lot of quarrelling and disunity amongst the children, and no group play; sometimes they shared a book and this would start quite happily with the children sitting beside each other and turning the pages together, but after a few minutes it inevitably ended in a squabble and tears. Sometimes, too, a nurse would put two children into one cot 'to play together' for a few minutes before being tucked down for the night in their own cots; these children then hugged and squeezed each other with frenzied enthusiasm. But there was no real unity or friendship amongst the children on either of the wards.

The staff/child communication was very poor, and revolved solely around the children's functional needs, i.e. going to the lavatory, eating or washing. Sometimes the children were attended to in absolute silence. One can make allowance for this, knowing that several of the Ridge Hospital nurses were working in England in order to learn the language, but one wonders whether it would not have been possible to have pointed out to young staff that small children require some form of communication.

The children got very little individual attention from the ward staff, except on the rare occasions when they had a much coveted 'turn' in the kitchen. Christopher, the deaf child, was not communicated with for hours at a stretch; this seemed especially sad, as a sign or a facial expression or a touch is life itself to a deaf child.

The fragmentation of care made individual attention difficult; for example, one nurse would undress a child, another wash him and perhaps a third would dry and dress him; this sort of routine made sustained individual attention quite impossible.

The staff did not participate in the children's play, and ward duties such as bed straightening or repetitive dusting came before the play demands of the children; children would sometimes be calling out for paper and pencils, and for books and cuddles, but the nurses were too busy completing their set rota of duties and so they did not respond to the children. During the one weekend on the ward only three brief examples of staff participation in play were noticed – one nurse played 'Ten little nigger boys' with a child as she dressed her in her cot, then she playfully chased her down the ward in her wheelchair; another nurse threw a ball twice to a child and then danced down the ward with that child in her arms; and another nurse let a little boy sit on a shelf in the linen cupboard for two or three minutes and he pretended it was his house.

The children were not given opportunities for independence, everything was done for them, and they took no part in chores, such as laying tables (the tables were not laid anyway) or in folding clothes up, or pouring drinks, or even in helping themselves to slices of bread and butter. Even their toothpaste was pressed out onto their toothbrushes for them; in the evening one could see a row of little toothbrushes in the bathroom, all standing in numbered tooth-mugs, each brush with a quarter-inch of paste on it, which had been squeezed out ready for the morning.

The lack of safety for toys was another disturbing feature of the ward life. The children often had to guard their toys quite fiercely in order to prevent them being snatched or broken by other children. The condition of ward possessions was often very poor, for example books were torn and grubby and often had pages missing.

The use of television was indiscriminate, and was used as a

means of occupying children whilst staff got others ready for bed. It was quite common for television programmes to stay on all through sport – wrestling, boxing, cricket, car-racing, horse-racing, football, and even lists of football results – with very little interest shown by the children sitting immobile before the set.

The numbering of personal belongings, such as toothbrushes, combs and tooth-mugs, one of the most out-dated practices of institutions and a particularly bad form of depersonalization, was a surprising thing to find in a children's ward in the 1960s. The staff themselves found difficulty in remembering the numbers and the whole idea served no purpose; but nobody on the staff thought to question the custom; the only explanation they could offer for its continuance was to say, 'It's always been done.'

Ridge Hospital gave the impression that it offered a very poor standard of child care and home-making. Many of the children in the ward did not need hospital care, but were in hospital because they needed schooling, a home and physiotherapy; indeed, their handicaps were sometimes much less complicated than were those of children who were managing to live adequately at home or in residential schools. It was very worrying to realize that these non-ill children did not live in this hospital for merely a matter of weeks, but for years, with the same old pattern of life being repeated each day. On similar visits paid to Ridge on other occasions, the same routines were going on for the same children, and the same distress was surging through the wards and the same anxiety was on the children's faces. Only the staff were different; they kept on changing.

3. Larchdale: a Residential School in the Suburbs

The school was on a hill surrounded by a well-populated residential area of pleasant suburban houses, with shops and station nearby. The school was run by a Voluntary Society with religious foundations; it accommodated approximately sixty boys and girls; twenty of the children were under five and lived in a separate building apart from the main school.

The children's handicaps were caused by spina bifida. They had disabilities and loss of sensation in the lower limbs, varying from severe to slight; some children had complications of bladder and bowel control. Many had had the operation of ileostomy, whereby a urine drainage bag from their abdomen saved them the social anxiety of wetting themselves and wearing nappies. It was necessary for the children to maintain very regular toilet habits, in order to see to the emptying of their bags and to cope with bowel incontinence; the risk of sores occurring in limbs that lacked sensation meant that a high standard of personal hygiene was necessary, with constant checks being made to ensure that, if a sore did occur, it could be dealt with promptly.

The children of Larchdale, unlike the children at Fieldway, were of normal or above-normal intelligence; and most of them were very secure in their family relationships. A few of the children were away with their parents during the summer week-end that I spent in the school.

The buildings had belonged to the Voluntary Society for some years and had been well-adapted to accommodate handicapped children. The entrance hall had glass front doors and was pleasantly furnished with easy chairs and a table. There were two main corridors, one upstairs and one downstairs. Both corridors were wide and allowed plenty of room for wheel-chairs. At the end of each corridor there was a staircase, and a lift in the entrance hall.

The corridor downstairs had bedrooms, bathrooms, classrooms, a physiotherapy room, recreation hall and headmaster's office leading off it. The corridor upstairs had classrooms, bedrooms and bathrooms, matron's office and a medical room leading off it. This mixing of classrooms, bedrooms and bathrooms had sometimes been criticized by both visitors and staff, but the idea was to allow easy access to the classrooms for children who might be confined to their beds because of recent operations or sore places.

The corridor upstairs was painted pink, the one downstairs pink and yellow. The downstairs corridor was also decorated with framed reproductions, children's art work and posters of animals and birds.

There were nine bedrooms, six bathrooms and four classrooms, a physiotherapy room, dining-room, recreation hall and garden. The younger children, those aged six, seven and eight, were accommodated in groups of five or more to a bedroom, but the older children, those of thirteen or fourteen plus, were in groups of two or three to a bedroom.

The bedrooms were all very individual in style, having family photographs on display, competition cups, personal ornaments, records, knick-knacks and books on the dressing-tables and lockers.

The dining-room, on the ground floor, was plain. It had four long tables in it, the younger children's table being lower than the others. Ten children could be seated round each table. The walls of the dining-room were blue. There were framed pictures on the walls, and heavy, good quality curtains at the long windows. The window-sills were broad and could be sat on; the radiators were small. A piano stood at one end of the dining-room.

The flooring throughout the whole school was good standard wood block, with tiled floors in the bathrooms.

The school garden had lovely rose-beds, a lawn, a paved play area just outside the french doors, and garden seats. There was a rabbit in a hutch under a rhododendron tree in the middle of the lawn.

A tree-lined drive led up to the school, from the busy main road. A short distance away there were several shops.

Staff

The staff of the school consisted of a matron and a sister, both being State Registered Nurses, and twelve 'nurse-housemothers'. During the week there were also teachers, clerical staff and physiotherapists.

The twelve nurse-houseparents were experienced or trained housemothers, young women who were gaining experience with children before starting training as houseparents or hospital nurses, or doing voluntary service, before going on to Colleges or University. These twelve members of staff were regarded as 'nurses' by the children, but were always called by their Christian names. The more senior of the twelve wore uniforms like those of hospital nurses. The matron and sister also wore nursing uniforms.

A night-nurse cared for the children during the night, being on duty from approximately 10 p.m. until 6.30 a.m. Night-care involved toileting and emptying of urine bags as necessary. Before going off duty in the mornings the night-nurse cooked breakfast for staff and children, but she was not responsible for serving any breakfast.

The day-staff duty times were arranged to be from 6.30 a.m. until 3 p.m., or from 2 p.m. until approximately 9.30 or 10 p.m. The staff had one whole day off per week, and took turns at doing 'split' duties. (Split duties meant starting at 6.30 a.m. as usual, then having a longer period off in the afternoon and working on until 9.30 or 10 p.m.)

The day-staff saw to the getting up of the children, which started at 6.45 a.m. on Saturdays and 7.30 on Sundays. Saturday breakfast was served between 7.45 and 8.15, and Sunday breakfast was served at 8.30 a.m.

Shortages of staff meant occasional lapping over of duty times, and some duty hours were readjusted for staff taking children for out-patient appointments, or for hospital visiting when children went for operations.

The twelve houseparents always kept to their own groups of children, having extra help from each other if necessary.

The shortage of staff also affected other parts of the domestic routine. During the week-end I spent at the school the house-parents were having to do the cooking, as there was only a part-time untrained cook on Saturdays and no cook at all on Sundays.

The staff had to do a lot of housework in addition to their work directly concerned with caring for the children. They had to sweep floors, dust, clean the bathrooms and toilets, wash floors, serve meals, hand-wash finer clothes, iron, clean the kitchen, cook, wash-up and prepare vegetables, and see to the bedrooms. Care of the children involved bathing, dressing, assisting with fixing of calipers, helping with toilet training, helping with care of urine drainage bags, organization of games and activities, escorting on outings, and, in general, acting as temporary parents.

The nature of the children's handicap meant that they did require a fair amount of knowledgeable nursing care, although this was not immediately obvious because they appeared so independent and able. However, several children in the school had undergone recent major surgery; there was the necessity of bowel training and adaptation to urine drainage bags; there was the issuing of drugs to combat infections and sores; and plasters, walking aids, calipers and intricate back braces to be coped with.

A Diary of a Week-end

The following is the diary of one week-end for six little girls in Larchdale School. They were aged between six and eight years, and all shared one bedroom (called here Bedroom One).

The girls were: Carol and Diane (eight) and Sally and Jean (seven), all of whom could get themselves around in wheelchairs. Josey (seven) was very twisted and very frail. She wore long calipers to her waist, as well as a back-brace. She walked slowly with arm-crutches. Lou (six) could walk, although her legs were twisted and weak.

All the girls except Lou had had the ileostomy operation. Lou wore nappies and plastic pants. Sally, one of the wheelchair girls, had her leg in plaster because of a recent orthopaedic operation.

All these girls were of normal intelligence.

The Saturday diary describes the day generally for these six children. The Sunday diary concentrates on Sally.

Saturday

At 6.30 a.m.: It was a hot summer morning and the six girls of Bedroom One were waking up. Mary, the nurse who looked after them, had drawn back the curtains and the girls were throwing off their bed-clothes and reaching out for toys or books, or were sitting up in bed waiting for their wheel-chairs to be brought to them. The whole house was quiet, but children could be heard dimly from other rooms, sleepily calling out to each other and moving around preparing to get dressed.

Bedroom One was on the first floor and had its own bathroom beside it. This bedroom was not in the main corridor but in a cul-de-sac at the top of the staircase, so it was rather secluded. There were no carpets, but high-standard wood-block flooring. The doors were very wide and sliding, allowing easy access for wheel-chairs.

Mary, the nurse for Bedroom One, was an unqualified girl of under twenty who was waiting to go to University. Her work at the school was under a system of volunteer service for which she was paid a small wage. She had worked there for several months.

Getting up in Bedroom One was very leisurely and slow; nobody seemed to be in a hurry and one or two of the girls slipped down into bed again and pulled up the sheets for another sleep.

By 7.20 a.m.: The girls had started getting to the bathroom in their wheel-chairs. They had heaved themselves into the wheel-chairs from their beds, as the chairs were brought to the bedsides.

Two girls were still on their beds playing with dolls, two were combing their hair at the dressing-tables, and two were in the bathroom with Mary. Bathroom procedures were very important for the children, necessitating the fixing of their drainage bags and their bowel training. They had to be in and out of the bathroom a lot during the day.

The bathroom was used solely by the six girls of Bedroom One. Inside were two low toilets with a wooden partition between them and folding doors. There was one wash-basin. Toothbrushes were in a holder above the basin, each toothbrush being named. The children helped themselves to toothpaste from a shared tube. On one wall were hooks and rails for flannels and towels, each hook named for a child.

A large sheet-covered table near the bath was used for helping the children who needed treatment for sores, etc., or for drying after bathing. The bath was away from the wall in order to give all-round help in bathing. A little stool was available for use in the bath for children to prop their leg on should they be in a plaster. Spare drainage bags for each child were hanging on the wall at the end of the bath.

Behind the two toilets were very wide window-sills on which ointments, powder and toothpaste were kept. Mirrors on the wall beside the toilets enabled the girls to inspect themselves for developing sores, so that prompt action could be taken to heal them. This early training in self-care in sore detection meant that the children grew up with an attitude of independence in coping with their handicap. The girls were allowed freedom to go in and out of the bathroom as they pleased and were encouraged to be independent.

By 7.45 a.m.: The girls were all ready and dressed and going down for breakfast. The last two off their beds had dressed themselves very quickly.

Lou, the youngest girl of the room, had walked slowly down the stairs, clinging on to the banisters. The others went down by lift, hurtling themselves at a good speed in their wheel-chairs along the corridor towards the lift. They were not allowed in the lift without a grown-up, so I went down with them. When inside the lift with the gates shut they said:

'Turn the lights out, make it dark.'

'We like it dark, go on, make it dark.'

Then they made loud eerie noises and there was a lot of giggling.

Down in the dining-room the tables were laid for breakfast. Some of the older children were gathered at one of the wide window-sills, looking at the post which was piled there for staff and children.

'Most of it is for Diane because it is her birthday,' one of the children said with envy. Diane was eight that day; she was one of the Bedroom One girls.

'Is this all mine?' she asked everybody.

The older boys and girls helped Diane to sort out her birthday post by reading the ones addressed to her.

At 8 a.m.: The younger children settled to their places at table and the older children served them with cereals as the staff arrived in the room with the trolley and hot breakfast. One of the older boys then said a short prayer and breakfast started.

The staff served the hot breakfast from a large plug-in electric trolley. Two staff served and the older boys carried the plates to each child. Other children arrived for breakfast during the following twenty minutes.

At 8.20 a.m.: Some children were still finishing breakfast, others had finished and were talking, or looking at their letters. Matron then came into the dining-room and gave a short semi-religious talk, stressing that the children should help each other as much as possible and remember not to judge others too harshly. Then she read out the list of duties for the week. These duties were dusting, laying-up tables, helping with sweeping and serving meals. Even the youngest children sometimes had a small duty concerned with the running of the school. It may only have been putting out mugs for the meals, but they were expected to keep to it.

At 8.55 a.m.: Five of the girls went back to the bedroom. Diane, the birthday girl, carried her parcels and letters with her. Matron had suggested that she took them upstairs so as to keep them safely.

One of the girls stayed down in the dining-room, chatting to some of the older boys. The staff did not expect her to break off her conversation and go back to Bedroom One with the others. There was no regimentation; children finished their breakfasts slowly and then wandered off casually wherever they wanted to go.

The girls in the bedroom busied themselves going to and from the bathroom and bedroom, washing their hands, wiping their faces with flannels, cleaning their teeth and going to the toilet. There was a lot of chatting, and much interest in Diane and her birthday cards. One card took all their attention: it was in the shape of a large highly coloured tiger, and had a game on the back of it. There was also a card in the form of a dog with a wobbly head; the girls stood this card on Diane's locker and took turns in wagging the head.

From 9.15 until 9.45 a.m.: The six girls played in their bedroom, or Mary helped them in the bathroom with their toilet training and drainage bags. Some of the girls thought they would tidy up their lockers, but these were so crammed with toys and bits and pieces that the children generally only looked at the collected treasures, then moved them to another shelf and shut the door. In the lockers there were old postcards, pencils, notebooks, dolls' clothes, odd badges, shaking games to get balls into holes, dolls and animals, board games, numerous ugly monkeys and other quaint hairy ugly animal shapes.

The lockers were wooden and had a drawer at the top and a door and two shelves underneath. On the top of each locker was a little mat, and more toys, pictures, photographs and ornaments.

The lockers were used mostly for toys and personal things. The girls' clothes were kept in large orange-painted built-in wardrobes. There were named partitions in the wardrobes for each girl and their dresses were hung on little hangers. Each girl also had her own drawer in one of the two dressing-tables where she kept vests, socks and pants. On the top of the dressing-tables were mats, picture postcards, birthday cards, combs, flowers and dolls. On one dressing-table there was a small aquarium of fish.

At 9.45 a.m.: The girls finished sorting out their lockers. They began to brush their hair and looked at themselves in the dressing-table mirrors. Lou, the youngest girl, took a chocolate box from her locker that was filled with different coloured ribbons and spent a long time selecting just the right colour to go with her gay dress. Then she very carefully rolled up all the ribbons and replaced the box in the locker.

At 9.50 a.m.: Three of the children went down to play in the garden. There were already groups of children playing there. One boy's bed had been pushed on to the concrete just outside the doors, and he was playing with a bat and ball.

Children were scattered over the building, in their bedrooms or reading in classrooms, some in the large recreation hall, some tidying up the remains of breakfast in the dining-room, and some playing in the garden.

Three of the Bedroom One girls were still in the bedroom, two were reading and colouring in books as they leaned on their beds from their wheel-chairs; the third child was having her calipers and brace fitted on. Matron came to help Mary fix the back brace, and she 'shooed' the other two out of the room: 'Go on out in the garden, it's a lovely day, you can't stay in on a day like this,' she rebuked them.

At 10 a.m.: All the girls were down in the garden, where they played in groups with the other children. The formation of play groups was spontaneous. Some played a coin game, tossing it and scoring for heads or tails. They were scrupulously fair in their score-keeping. Another group played marbles. At one point they tired of the conventional rolling game because their handicaps made it difficult. Instead they threw all the marbles into the rose-garden, and then made up a complicated search game amongst the lumps of soil around the rose-bushes. Some children played 'tennis' with the boy in bed. The ages mixed in the games, although sometimes the younger children were only very grudgingly admitted to a game with the older boys.

At 10.35 a.m.: I went into the kitchen and found Lou eating a thick slice of bread and Marmite. Her chin was almost on the kitchen table as she sat with her long thin legs wound round the legs of a big chair. Dinner was being prepared by the temporary cook. Jean, another Bedroom One girl, was helping to carry tins of carrots from the draining board to the table where Lou quietly munched her bread and Marmite.

'How many tins will we want? Just one?' Jean asked the cook.

'No, that won't go far now, will it?'

'If we only have one tin, how much will we have each?' asked Jean.

'Only a tiny bit.'

'A bit as big as a match,' giggled Jean. She fetched all six tins, one by one, from the draining board, carrying the tins on her lap and wheeling herself deftly with one hand.

Lou watched intently as the cook smeared fat on chops and placed them in a huge baking tin.

From 11 until 11.15 a.m.: Sally was playing the piano alone in the dining-room. Another girl was in the bathroom and three were in the bedroom. Jean was still in the kitchen. The three girls in the bedroom had just been told that they had been invited to a party at a nearby College that afternoon. They decided to change their clothes and chose dresses they would be able to wear to the party.

From 11.15 until 11.45 a.m.: All six girls were in the garden again. The boy on the bed was playing with a pair of sunglasses. He had three large rolls of different coloured cellophane and he was cutting out circles of cellophane and sticking them on to his glasses to make varied tints.

Other children had organized themselves into a large group with balls.

'I know, I know, let's play schools, oh, do let's play schools.'

'Where is my score-card, somebody has got my score-card,' shouted one boy.

'I'm going into the kitchen to see if dinner is nearly ready,' said another boy.

Just before 12: Sally and Carol were in the dining-room. Sally was playing the piano again, whilst Carol was bustling up and down in her wheel-chair looking for clean mugs to put on the tables for lunch. This was her duty for the day, but she was a little worried because she could not find the mugs. She went into the scullery and found the mugs on the draining-board, not yet wiped up from breakfast time. She wiped them up, took them back into the dining-room, balanced on a tray on her wheelchair, and then put them round the tables. An older boy then came in with a full jug of water and Carol filled the mugs. Sally continued to play the piano.

At 12.15 p.m.: The dinner bell was rung and all the younger children came in and sat down for lunch. On the tables were cruets, knives, forks and spoons, mugs for water, mats and paper napkins. Three members of staff served the meal from the plugged-in trolley which was wheeled in from the kitchen. One of the older boys who could walk helped to take the plates round to the children. Grace was said before starting. Some of the older children came in late. All the children ate with knives and forks, the younger ones having help with cutting up their meat. Talking was allowed but not too much shouting. Two of the staff ate their own meal with the children, one sitting with the older children and one with the younger group. The rest of the staff had their lunch in the staff-room.

As the children finished lunch they went into the garden again, or up to their bedrooms. They did not wait all together until all had finished, because some children were slow eaters and others had come in late.

At 1.20 p.m.: The six girls were in Bedroom One, getting themselves ready for the party. They chose their dresses, talking about the colours and matching them carefully with ribbons from their ribbon boxes which they emptied on to their beds. Two of the girls were bathed by Mary.

From 2.20 until 2.35 p.m.: The children going to the party waited by the porch for the van-driver to help them into the school-van. All the Bedroom One girls were going, as well as a child from another bedroom. The van-driver worked at the school. He knew the children very well and he joked with them when he came to load them into the van; it was a tight squeeze to get in all the wheel-chairs, the children and the three helpers.

By 2.45 p.m.: The last child was packed into the van, and, with one helper at the back and two in front with the driver, they set off on the short drive through the suburbs. At one point the driver pulled into the kerb and turned round to grumble at the girls because they were hanging their hands from the van windows. They continued the journey in a subdued silence.

At 3 p.m.: They arrived at the College where the party was held. There were slides and see-saws on the vast lawns, and games with balls. Under the trees was a collection of pets, guinea-pigs, rabbits, gerbils, a parrot and a tortoise. The handicapped children found these pets a big attraction, and they were allowed to nurse the tortoise on their laps as they sat in their wheel-chairs in the shade. They also spent a long time stroking the largest rabbit. At one end of the grounds there was a small lake and one or two of the group were taken for a short ride in a boat.

There were children at the party from other homes and schools in the area, but these were not physically handicapped. There was also a small group of elderly people from a local Over-Sixties Club, who sat on the College terrace in the shade.

Before having tea at small tables in the big hall the children were taken to the toilet by their helpers who had come with them, and they had their urine bags emptied. After tea the students at the College put on a children's play in the garden.

At 6 p.m.: They left the College. It was quite difficult to get Diane back to the van because she had attached herself to three students and was chatting about her birthday. Diane was convinced that this very large party had been entirely in honour of her own birthday and the students kindly let her believe this.

On the way home in the van there was a lot of spontaneous noisy singing of 'Daisy, Daisy, give me your answer, do' and the children made up variations of this by substituting the names of school staff for 'Daisy'.

At 6.20 p.m.: They arrived back at the school. Carol and Jean went to the lift and immediately up to the bathroom to empty their urine bags.

At 6.30 p.m.: Lou, the youngest girl, went up to Bedroom One and told the others: 'We must stay up here now to get ready for bed.'

From 6.30 until 7.30 p.m.: All the Bedroom One girls were getting ready for bed. They played with water in the bathroom, putting the plug in the basin, filling the basin until the water went down the over-flow and then rushing on to the landing in their wheel-chairs, shouting out: 'This is an emergency, a flood, a flood, everybody, emergency!'

In the middle of their undressing the girls had biscuits, fruit drinks and potato crisps from a tray, which was brought up for them by one of the staff. There was quite a bit of bouncing up and down on the beds and rushing about in wheel-chairs, and crisps were grabbed excitedly from the tray.

Diane, who had been given a tube of bubble-bath liquid for her birthday, squeezed a generous portion of this on to each girl's hand and they hurried into the bathroom to make bubbles on their hands. The large tiger birthday card was suddenly the cause of a quick quarrel as another child took it. Diane shrieked that it was her 'very best of all birthday card' and it was quickly given back.

Carol, who was still getting used to having a urine drainage bag, kept going round to the others and anxiously asking them if they thought it was fixed all right or was it leaking.

One girl helped Carol and felt her clothes to see if they were damp and reassured her that all was well, but another child was exasperated by Carol's continual worrying and snapped at her: 'Really, it's quite all right, you keep fussing, fussing, all day long, you silly.' Carol wheeled herself out of the bathroom to check with Mary if everything really was safe with her bag.

During this time of undressing the girls were assisted in the bedroom and bathroom by Mary, and occasionally by another older houseparent who was working in a bedroom farther along the corridor. The children folded up their underwear as well as they could. The boots and calipers were placed under the beds by Mary, the dresses were put back on their hangers in the fitted cupboards if they were clean enough to be worn another day. The wheel-chairs were placed in the corridor.

At 7.30 p.m.: The curtains were drawn to, and each child was settled down and tucked in for the night. They were still excited and kept laughing.

'Mary, Mary,' they called out.
'Come on, Mary, give me my good-night kiss.'
'Are we having a lie-in in the morning?'
'Is it really Sunday tomorrow?'
'Ice cream and jelly, a punch in the belly.'
'Oh, did you hear what she said, Mary?'
'You forgot to kiss me good night, come back.'

Each child was given a good-night kiss by Mary. As she went out of the room there was some more giggling and pretending that she had missed some of them out. They tried to call her back. The door was pulled half-way to. The girls, each with a doll or cuddly toy beside them, settled very quickly to sleep.

Sunday (A diary of Sally from Bedroom One)

Just after 7.30 a.m.: On a dull Sunday morning Sally got out of bed and went to the bathroom. She had got herself from her bed into her wheel-chair after it had been brought to her bedside by Mary. She wheeled herself quickly to the bathroom and washed. Then she emptied her urine bag and lifted herself from her wheel-chair on to the toilet.

At 7.45 a.m.: Sally washed her hands and went back to the

bedroom and opened the wardrobe. She took some time to choose a dress, sitting staring thoughtfully into the wardrobe. In the middle of deciding about her dress she wandered away from the cupboard and joined in a maze-game on the back of the tiger-shaped birthday card that had caused so much interest in the bedroom on Saturday.

By 8.15 a.m.: Sally had finally chosen her dress and asked the approval of Mary. She put it on and Mary helped her with the fastening at the back. Then she sat in front of the dressing-table mirror, combing her hair and talking. Next she chose a ribbon from her ribbon box. She wanted to match her dress, predominantly green and yellow. After great deliberations she chose a speckled ribbon, holding it up for the other girls to approve.

At 8.30 a.m.: Sally went down to the dining-room and helped herself to a huge helping of grapefruit segments from a bowl in the centre of her table. She sat at the end of her table because her plastered leg was stuck out at an awkward angle from her wheelchair.

Grace was said and breakfast begun. The older girls and boys were not in this dining-room for breakfast as they were having their breakfast in the small sitting-room off the entrance hall. But one of the older boys came through and helped with the serving of breakfast.

Sally took until 9 o'clock to finish her breakfast, then she stayed in the dining-room chatting to the other children while they finished.

At 9.15 a.m.: Sally went upstairs in the lift. She went to the bathroom, cleaned her teeth and went to the toilet. The other girls of Bedroom One were in the bathroom with her. There was a sudden great interest in talking about photographs of their parents. The children said: 'Wait up here and when we've finished we'll show you our photos of our mummies.'

From 9.35 until 9.55 a.m.: Sally sat on the toilet, calling out to another girl who was on the toilet on the other side of the partition.

At 10.10 a.m.: Sally went down to the entrance hall, after having taken a short while to tidy her hair ready for Church.

From 10.20 until 10.40 a.m.: Sally sat in the entrance hall looking at the Sunday newspaper colour supplements. She read out the adverts and tried to read the captions under the pictures. Suddenly seeing an advertisement for tinned milk, depicting a tin cut in half to a shape resembling a crown, Sally and her particular friend Carol had a quick game about which crown they would choose. They pulled haughty faces and sat up very straight in their wheel-chairs and pretended they were queens.

A group of about twelve children were in the hall at this time, moving around in their wheel-chairs or looking at books or newspapers as they waited for others to get ready and the van-driver to take them to the Church. Some would go to the Church in the van, but others would be pushed down by Youth Club members. It was trying to rain and quite dark outside.

At 10.40 a.m.: Sally went outside because the slight drizzle of rain had stopped and some of the children were being loaded into the van.

Sally wheeled herself quickly round to the passenger seat and played with a length of rope which the children already in the van threaded out to her from the open window. The rope was long and she wound it around her wheel-chair and then urged the others to send out more. They found another length and flung that out, laughing and shouting to Sally. This last length of rope fell on Sally's head and she wheeled herself swiftly round to the back of the van and threw the rope back through the open doors on to the children who sat inside. The van-driver suddenly appeared from the house to put Sally in the van.

'I know what I'll do with you,' he said as he untangled Sally and her chair from pieces of rope. He pretended to tie her up and then lifted her up into the van with the other children.

'We'll tie *you* up,' the children chorused at him as he shut the doors of the van.

At 10.50 a.m.: They went off to Church.

In the house the staff were busy sweeping bedrooms and corridors, washing drainage bags, tidying up the bedrooms, cooking, and washing down the stairs. The children left in the house were not disturbed by the tidying up; the atmosphere was rather like that of a large family with an overworked mother very busy and the children doing their bit towards getting Sunday dinner ready.

At 12.20 p.m.: The children returned from Church. They went into the dining-room after chatting for a while in the entrance hall and taking off their coats. A member of staff took the coats upstairs and put them away.

At 12.35 p.m.: The children were in the dining-room, sitting down for lunch; it was being served from the trolley and given out by a senior boy and two staff members. Grace was said before starting. Again, two of the staff ate their own lunch with the children, one sitting with the youngest children, the other at the middle table.

At 1.25 p.m.: Sally finished her lunch and then played in the corridor for a while, wheeling herself slowly up and down and talking to a boy who was in bed. His bed had been wheeled along the corridor to the open dining-room door, so that he had lunch with the others. He was looking at comics as he finished off his lunch from a tray on his bed.

At 1.40 p.m.: Sally went up to the bedroom with the other girls from her room. She went to the toilet and washed her hands. She said: 'My dad wears false teeth. My dad and mum are coming to see me this afternoon.'

Lou, the youngest girl of Bedroom One, came into the bathroom and practised dance steps in a frail wobbly fashion across the bathroom floor. Sally told her that she was doing it all wrong.

'No, do your arms like *this*, Lou,' Sally said kindly.

Sally and Carol tried to instruct Lou. They stretched their arms above their heads as they sat in their wheel-chairs and they waved their hands gracefully while Lou watched intently and tried to imitate their movements.

Another houseparent was helping the children in the bathroom at this moment because Mary was off duty for a couple of hours.

At 1.55 p.m.: 'Let's go and play games,' said Sally.

Carol and Sally wheeled themselves towards the lift. It was pouring with rain and there was no chance of getting into the garden

'Shall we get some games from matron?'

'No, matron's off. This will do,' replied Carol. She had a toy doctor's bag of bright red plastic and she clutched this tightly on her lap as she wheeled herself rapidly towards the lift with Sally following.

On their way past the dining-room the two girls found a boy slowly finishing his lunch on his own. They went into the dining-room with self-righteous cries of horror at his slowness. Leaning across the table they lectured him and threatened that he would get into trouble.

At 2.5 p.m.: Carol and Sally went into the sitting-room. This was a small room, decorated in blue, and with wall settees and chairs and tables in it. There was also a bookcase, pictures on the walls, shelves of books and magazines, and an aquarium of fish. This was the room in which the older children had eaten their breakfast.

'We call this room the sitting-room, *not* a lounge,' Sally explained.

She then left Carol with the doctor's bag and sat in a corner of the room on her own and quickly became interested in a book.

Carol started to get the doctor game ready on her own. The other children in the room looked across, stopped what they were doing, and took over the doctor's set from Carol.

'Let's play out-patients,' the children said.

'Oh, yes,' answered Carol excitedly.

'We have hurt our arms.'

'No, we've got to have operations.'

'We must have medicine.'

'Bags I give the injections.'

There was loud arguing as all the children wanted to be noisy upset out-patients rather than quiet doctors, then shouts of 'No, no' as they pretended to have their arms injected.

At 2.20 p.m.: Sally finished reading and silently left the sitting-room, showing no interest in the doctor game. She wheeled herself into the dining-room, which was then empty, and played the piano.

At 2.35 p.m.: Sally looked out of the long windows of the dining-room and saw her parents' car arriving through the pouring rain.

At 2.40 p.m.: Sally was in the sitting-room with her parents, having hurried into the hall to meet them. Other parents and children were also arriving. A small group of children still played a noisy game of out-patients in one corner of the sitting-room and some of the visiting children joined in.

Children and parents and brothers and sisters were now scattered throughout the house and school, some in bedrooms, some in classrooms and corridors, others in the recreation hall and the dining-room.

From 2.40 p.m. onwards: Sally was with her family, her mother nursing on her lap one of the children who had not got a visitor. Sally coloured the books that her mother had brought for her.

The children in the corner of the sitting-room still played out-patients. Some bowls of water had been fetched from the bathroom to make the game more realistic and this was spilt on to the chair as the children pretended to struggle against injections.

At 3 p.m.: It was drink time. Drinks and biscuits and shortbread slices were served in the hall from the trolley, some children helped themselves and others had it brought to them by the staff. The visitors had their tea and biscuits brought into the sitting-room for them and they shared it with the children around them.

The boy who was confined to his bed was in the corridor just outside the sitting-room. His bed had been continually wheeled around the house all the week-end to wherever there was something interesting going on.

From 3.15 p.m. onwards: The group of visitors and children in the sitting-room played guitars, talked, did puzzles and coloured painting books. The visiting parents frequently took children on to their laps, not always the ones they had come to visit.

At 3.30 p.m.: Lou's parents came. She went to the front door and let them in and they went up to the bedroom with her to see something she had to show them. Visiting parents moved freely around the house according to what the children wanted to show them.

From 3.45 until 4.45 p.m.: Some younger children who did not have visitors played snakes and ladders with one of the houseparents in a room adjoining the staff-room.

At 4.45 p.m.: The parents started to leave and the staff made preparations for a service to be held in the recreation hall. Chairs were placed in rows in front of the piano and children came in as they were ready. They either sat on the chairs or found a space in a row for their wheel-chairs.

From 5 until 5.45 p.m.: The service took place. It was given by visitors connected with the local Church. When the service finished Sally stayed behind in the hall and talked to three young people from the United States who had sung at the service. One of these American visitors had a guitar and Sally was interested in this. Other children began to go to the dining-room for supper.

At 6 p.m.: Supper time. The staff served the supper which was a hot savoury one: sausages, tomatoes, etc. Sally did not go in to supper until 6.15 as she was still talking to the Americans.

Diane cut her birthday cake, helped by a houseparent because it was so new and crumbly. The cook had made it for her, but she hadn't cut it on Saturday because of going to the party.

Before Diane cut the cake everybody sang 'Happy Birthday' and she blew out the eight candles.

'I blew them all out in one blow,' she called excitedly to everyone.

Then at 6.45 p.m.: Sally went up to the bedroom. She played with her dolls, pretending they were having operations on their stomachs. She had a candle-holder from Diane's birthday cake, and she pretended this was a needle. Suddenly a piece of this candle-holder got stuck into the middle of her doll's stomach and then broke off.

'Quick, an emergency, find me an operating table,' shouted Sally, rushing herself along in her wheel-chair to the bathroom, carrying the doll.

Carol and Sally peered closely at the doll's stomach, giggling and then looking very serious.

'Whatever is it?' asked Carol.

'A piece of that candle-thing from Diane's cake,' wailed Sally. 'Oh, I don't think it will ever come out.'

'Look, Mary, look what happened,' Sally said to her nurse, holding up the doll.

'Well, you are a silly, you have spoilt the doll now,' said Mary. 'Get undressed and ready for bed, we'll see to it later.'

From 7.15 until 7.40 p.m.: Sally hurried quickly through her toileting, washing and undressing, so that she could get back to her doll.

From 7.40 until 7.55 p.m.: Sally was ready for bed and in her nightdress, sitting on her bed and silently concentrating on her doll's stomach. Other children were getting into bed, or being helped by Mary in the bathroom, or were sitting in bed playing with dolls and reading.

'I've done her operation and she mustn't sit up yet,' announced Sally in a loud pleased voice. She laid the doll carefully on the top of her locker. The other children all looked up with interest.

'Is she better?' they asked.

'Not yet, but she will be feeling better in the morning.'

Sally covered the doll with a little cloth.

At 8 p.m.: The six girls were tucked down, kissed good night and the curtains were drawn. There was a sudden little excitement and noise and an older houseparent came from along the corridor and said they must settle down and stop being noisy. Quietly the door was pushed half-to, and the children settled to sleep cuddling their soft toys.

Impressions of Larchdale

Comparing the children with spina bifida who lived in Larchdale School to those who lived at Ridge Hospital, it is astonishing to realize that two groups of similarly handicapped children can live such different lives. A freak of chance placed seven-year-old Sally in Larchdale School and eight-year-old Tony in Ridge Hospital, and they subsequently lived utterly contrasting lives although they had the same handicaps. Sally was able to get out, in a garden, to Church, to a party, she had many rooms to play in, she was able to be alone, she helped with household chores and watched her food cooked; she was in a group of children of mixed ages and she had her own housemother. But Tony spent his life in one bed-filled upstairs room, he did not have any one particular adult to care for him, he never saw his food cooked, he was not even permitted to wheel his chair out on to the landing by the drinks kitchen.

Chance residential placement gave Sally a rich, secure and

interesting life, and Tony an insecure and empty life in one room. The effects of opportunity, or lack of opportunity, in childhood are felt all through life; there can be no going back to re-claim the wasted life — Sally's childhood in Larchdale School would enable her to get a job and a home of her own later on, but Tony's childhood in Ridge Hospital was fitting him only for a life-long existence in an institution (perhaps a geriatric ward or a hospital for the chronically disabled and retarded).

Another outstanding impression at Larchdale was the amount of room that the children had, and their freedom to move around unsupervised. There was no restriction of space, and every opportunity to be alone and make use of bedrooms, bathroom, schoolrooms, dining-room, kitchen and garden. In the week-end diary of Sally and her friends it is recorded that she frequently took herself off to play the piano alone and other children absorbed themselves in quietly sorting out ribbon boxes, drawers, etc. They were always free to get away from other children and were not harassed by noisy over-crowded community life. The environment was very pleasant, too, with colourful décor, cupboards and dressing-tables.

The children of Larchdale were very responsible; they had household duties and shared in the running of the home at weekends. The staff openly encouraged kindliness and service to others: this attitude may have been influenced by the religious principles underlying the original foundations of the school. The relationship between the children and staff at Larchdale was akin to that found in any large family. Several of the younger untrained housemothers were little older than the senior pupils of the school, and were more like older sisters than child-care staff; e.g. a senior girl poked her head from her bedroom door and shouted to one of the younger staff, 'Hey, lend me a shampoo until next week, can you?' And, on the Sunday morning, when senior children were playing records loudly in their bedrooms one of the younger staff, still in her nightdress, ran down from her own bedroom and asked the children to be quieter because she was having a lie-in. This relationship of independence and equality between children and staff was evident throughout the school; even the youngest children had a self-responsible air of independence.

The duties of the adults at Larchdale did not interfere with the activities of the children; and the adults were never so preoccupied with work that the children were made to feel in the way. The children were often in the kitchen, chatting and helping the staff with small jobs. There were no rules that children must keep out of the kitchen, except that the younger ones had to stay away from the tables or ovens when there was hot food about. All the children were well aware of food preparations, cooking smells and messes; this was a contrast to long-stay hospitals where children may not realize that a potato has a brown skin or that a sausage starts off being pink.

At no time did the children of Larchdale have to spend hours waiting for things to be done. Because of the nature of their handicaps the children did have to spend a fair amount of time in and out of the bathrooms and toilets, but this procedure was never made a burden and no child was kept waiting in a line until other children had been seen to *en masse*.

There was no evidence of children being 'chased' by staff primarily concerned with fulfilling duties. There was no unnecessary repetition of domestic duties, such as constant turning down of bed covers, or dusting of lockers.

The staff at Larchdale made efforts to see that less able children were not left out of group games; a child confined to his bed was pushed around the school so that he could take part in activities that were taking place in the dining-room and the garden. And the staff played with children who did not have visitors.

The children not only had changes of scene within their school premises, but they also had opportunities for going out, to functions in the neighbourhood, to Church, and so on. And the local Church Youth Club members visited the school.

There was no evidence of institutional mannerisms, such as repetitive anxious questioning of adults, hand-flapping and waving, head-banging or nodding, or aimless pushing up and down of single objects. The Larchdale children, unlike the children at Ridge, never kept calling, 'Lady, lady, come to me.'

The mixing of age groups in Larchdale was a particular advantage which is not always found in hospitals, where the children are often segregated according to age. There was plenty of reciprocation of services between younger and older children; younger children fetched things for the older ones, and the older ones helped the little ones at meal times or up and down stairs with their walking aids and so on. In this way, children experienced the care that they would find in any large family.

Despite the amount of housework that the Larchdale staff had to get through, the children were not deprived of attention. They needed vigilant physical care due to the nature of their handicap; this care bordered on nursing care, but there was no feeling of physical frailty or sickness within the school. Instead, there was a lot of freedom and the children showed the advantage of this by their independent behaviour and the responsible way in which they helped in the running of the school.

4. 'Blue Ward': A Week-end for Children with Severe Mental Disabilities

The final observations were made at a hospital which had some wards for children with severe mental disabilities and some wards for mentally able children who had physical illnesses. The two types of handicaps were not accommodated together. I spent a week-end there in late summer, working as a 'voluntary nurse' in a building which accommodated approximately fifty children who had been assessed as severely subnormal. The three-floored building had four main wards, separation rooms, kitchen, sister's offices, sluice rooms, bathrooms, toilets, staff cloakrooms and 'day' rooms. The physically able of the fifty retarded children lived on the ground and first floors, but the children who had severe physical handicaps in addition to their mental disabilities lived on the top floor. I worked in a ward on the top floor, here referred to as 'Blue Ward'.

'Blue Ward' had accommodation for eleven children. When I worked there, one child had been taken home for the weekend, leaving five girls and five boys aged from three to fourteen years. All these children were severely physically disabled, as well as having been classified as mentally subnormal. They could not hold anything, nor could they feed, wash or dress themselves. They could not speak; they were also doubly incontinent. Three of the children were blind, some were possibly deaf. Most were highly susceptible to chest infections; one little boy had a serious kidney complaint; one girl had a microcephalic skull, and one or two of the others had slight deformities of the skull. There were also one or two who had epilepsy. The children were utterly dependent upon the full-time everlasting care of other people; were they not washed, changed regularly, fed, kept warm and dry and given the appropriate medicine, they would soon develop sores and infections and die of malnutrition and pneumonia.

The five older children were in beds down one side of Blue Ward, and the five younger ones were in cots on the opposite side. All the children had bed cradles to prevent sheet pressures on their legs. Their names and religions were written on the end of their beds and cots. The beds and cots, about four feet apart, were in two straight rows down the ward. Each child had a wooden locker, which had a rail at the back for a large and a small towel. Inside some of the lockers were spare nightclothes, or baby toys, e.g. plastic rings; one locker had a birthday card in it with the words 'To a Dear Grandson'. Several lockers were completely empty.

The walls were painted shiny yellow, the floor tiled green. At one end of the ward was the fire-escape door, and a block of small grey metal lockers; these lockers were named and contained a few personal clothes. The hot-water pipes around the walls were covered in thick yellow-painted wire. There was a small wash-basin at one end of the room, and at the other end were two blue plastic-covered chairs designed for sitting disabled children in.

There were nine windows, five of them with thin curtains, now faded but originally printed with a nursery pattern; all the windows had lace curtains half-way up. The view from the windows was of tree-tops and the hospital walls, but the children could not see out anyway, as they were lying down all day and their beds were facing the centre of the ward.

The rails of the beds and cots were grey. The counterpanes were hospital type, of pink and blue, with nursery rhyme pictures and alphabets on them, faded with much laundering. A large floppy knitted doll was tied on the side of one cot. This belonged to seven-year-old Lu-Lu, who was cerebral palsied. One or two soft baby-toys were standing on the ends of some of the beds. There were no pictures in the room, nor ornaments, flowers, books, carpet, piano, radio, television, mats on the lockers, nor a toy cupboard.

I started work on the Saturday at 9 o'clock. The children were lying in their beds and cots, being fed their breakfast. One full-time nurse and one part-time nurse were on duty. Both these nurses were middle-aged married women who lived at home; the part-time nurse was unqualified and had worked in the hospital for about nine months; the full-time nurse was State Enrolled and had worked there for about nine years, always in the building for severely subnormal children.

The duty hours for a full-time nurse were from 7.30 a.m. until 7.30 p.m., with three-quarters of an hour for lunch, and fifteen minutes in the morning and the afternoon for a tea or coffee break. Full-time nurses usually worked four days in a row and then had three days off, and did occasional week-ends. To help solve problems of staff shortage the hospital permitted part-time nurses to arrange their work hours to suit their families.

The system in the building for the severely subnormal was for each nurse to go to a different ward each day; they did not know until they arrived in the morning which group (or ward) the sister had decided for them that day. The nurses said that the reason for this daily change was to share the load of heavy lifting and difficult children. It was also explained that a reason for the twelve-hour day was to prevent the comings and goings of 'split duties' – it was thought that if a nurse spent a whole twelve hours with one group of children then those children would have the advantage of seeing that one face all day. There appear to be some contradictions in these systems of going to a fresh ward every day and working twelve hours at a stretch: if a nurse was moved each day and did four days on and three days off, then her chances of getting back to the same group of children twice in one week were small; by the time she got round to the first group again she must have been virtually a stranger to them once more, despite her previous twelve-hour duty with them.

I started that Saturday by helping to finish feeding the children. This took us until 10 o'clock. The night-staff did not feed the children. When the day-staff arrived at 7.30 they usually began by washing and changing some of the children, until the breakfast came up from the kitchen at about 8 o'clock. Then feeding started and sometimes went on until 10 o'clock, depending on how many staff were available.

Feeding took a long time as each child had to be spoon-fed; some could not swallow properly and very few could chew their food; some children had difficulty in tongue control and food was liable to be brought back more often than swallowed. Everybody wore long white gowns when feeding because the children sometimes kept spitting food or coughing out their food. However, in spite of the difficulties, feeding was always persevered with, so the children received proper nourishment. Each child had all his breakfast on one plate – bacon, cereal, egg, and a spoonful of honey and milk on the top – and we mixed it all together into a pap. The children remained lying in their cots and beds, but we lifted them up slightly on to their pillows to make it a little easier for them to swallow.

As we fed the children, the two nurses chatted to each other and explained the ward routines to me. They said the children did not have to be lifted on to bedpans or carried out to the toilets, but had their nappies changed five times during the twenty-four hours. The ten children in Blue Ward would not have to be dressed because they stayed in their beds and cots all day. On a week-day, however, they told me, the children sometimes went to physiotherapy, or downstairs, and sometimes there was a clinic and the doctors came round. Some of the more physically able children in the downstairs wards went to a school-room, where they listened to the record-player and 'did things with beads and colours and things'.

Another reason for not attempting to dress the children was because there were several staff off sick; there was also a bazaar in the hospital grounds and most of the nurses wanted to spend a few moments over there. What with the bazaar, and three staff off sick, it was felt that putting the children into clothes would simply have added to the day's complications: 'Anyway, after all, if they *are* put into clothes we only put them straight back into bed again, that is all they can do, so it's a bit silly, isn't it, really? Sticking them in dresses and shirts and putting them under bedclothes again, it's hot for them, too.'

Asking if each child had his own wheel-chair, I was told that there were some wheel-chairs downstairs and sometimes the children in Blue Ward might go down. During the two days I spent on Blue Ward only the four children who had visitors were taken out of the room; the others spent the entire two days in bed.

After we had finished feeding the children we piled up the dirty dishes on a table on the landing and these were taken down in the lift to be washed up in the kitchen. The food for this building was cooked in a kitchen on the ground floor, sent to the wards in a heated trolley and left on the landings for the plates of food to be collected by ward nurses as required.

At 10 o'clock, two of us went for a tea-break and, when we returned at 10.15, we started washing the children. It took three of us until 11.15 to wash the ten children. We washed them all over, changed their nappies and gave them clean nightdresses if necessary.

Most of the children had wet nappies and their nighties were stained with food, so they needed completely changing. The children's contracted limbs and uncontrollable movements made it difficult to put on their nighties and nappies. The children did not have their own flannels for face and bodies; instead, we used strong paper napkins that were thrown away afterwards. As we finished each child we put on a clean draw sheet if necessary, tidied up the bed-clothes, and tucked them down again. The dirty linen was put into a bucket, or dirty linen container, ready for the laundry.

As we washed the children we helped ourselves to stainless steel wash-bowls, soap, paper flannels, powder, clean nighties and sheets from a trolley in the middle of the ward. We stood the washing bowls on the children's lockers as we washed them. A drawer in the trolley contained the only hair-brush, made of very strong nylon; the children shared this.

As we worked we talked about the difficulties of looking after the children, how they were being extra awkward to dress, how they smelt; at times, the nurses chivvied the children, saying, 'They know, they know.'

One of the little girls, six-year-old Freda, was expected to go home for one night, so she was dressed and sat in one of the blue chairs. But nobody knew what time her mother was coming, so a dinner was ordered for her in case she did not go until the afternoon. Freda sat smiling in the chair, and made excited little cries when we told her that 'mother's coming'.

Between just after 11.15 and 12 o'clock we had a relaxed time. We stood and talked in the ward and tidied up a few clothes in the linen cupboard. One of the nurses 'set-up' the trolley ready for the afternoon washing session, and I cleaned out the washing-bowls and dried them on paper towels. The other nurse leant over Lu-Lu's cotside and made coo-ing noises to her. Lu-Lu smiled up appreciatively.

The nurses explained how shortages of staff were not so acute in the weeks from autumn until Christmas, because people were looking for work then in order to get extra money for Christmas. 'It's not right, really, no it isn't,' explained one nurse indignantly. 'They only does it for Christmas money. I've been here nine years or more and I've seen it happen so many times now. They comes along, gets measured for uniform and all, then works up to Christmas, never says nothing about not staying, in fact gives you to believe they'll stay for years and years. Then, bang, come Christmas week and they say, "We're off, we've earnt ourselves a packet for Christmas". Bang, just like that! There we are, just at Christmas, no staff. Terrible it is the week after Christmas, only the oldtimers left, the others all gone, and double work for us.'

At 12 o'clock we started to feed the children their dinners. They had mashed potato, meat and carrots, and we mixed it well up into a pap for them. This time we sat down to feed, on long plastic-covered benches which were kept under the beds when not in use. We put bibs and paper napkins under the children's chins and over their chests, and afterwards the soiled bibs were sent to the laundry.

All the children were supposed to finish their first course before being given the sweet courses. Some of the children were very difficult to feed, clenching their teeth so that we could not get the spoons into their mouths, or else sending their food back again because of their swallowing problems. One child was so difficult that the nurse feeding her decided to hold her nose to make her swallow.

The nurses said that breakfast feeding was the easiest because the children were hungry first thing in the morning. Lunch was always difficult because it was quite early and the children had not long finished their breakfast. I was told that, if any of the children really could not manage all the food, I was to use my own discretion about leaving it. Some of the children preferred puddings to savouries; the nurses knew the children and understood their likes and dislikes about food – they said not to worry if one little boy I was feeding did not eat all his meat course as he was certain to eat all his custard.

At 12.15 the full-time nurse went to lunch. The part-timer and I stayed in Blue Ward to carry on feeding. The part-time nurse did not take a lunch-hour as she only worked until 3 o'clock, and then had lunch at home. At 1.15 the full-time nurse returned and I went for lunch. In one hour I had only managed to feed three children their meat course.

At 2 o'clock I returned to Blue Ward and found that the two nurses had just finished feeding the children. The part-time nurse then went home. It was then time to give the children their drinks; we used baby mugs with lids on them, and propped the children up slightly on their pillows, but the swallowing problems made drinking difficult.

At 2.30 we had a few minutes off to go to the bazaar and we hurried away across the grounds. Blue Ward would be looked after for a while by a nurse from the opposite ward. Before going, we put Freda back into her cot as we concluded her mother was not coming after all. But we left Freda's dress on in case mother turned up later. Freda's earlier excitement had petered away and she cried a little as she was put back into her cot.

At 3 o'clock we returned to the building. I went up to Blue Ward, but the other nurse went to look after another ward so that those nurses could have their turn at the bazaar. Left on my own in Blue Ward, I sat down on one of the benches to watch that the children were all right.

'Don't worry, there's nothing to do, just keep watch. If you need any of us, we're not far away,' I was told.

All the children were quietly tucked into their beds and cots. It was hard to believe that the blind children were unable to see, they were awake and had alert expressions and seemed to look intently round the room. Two of the sighted children dozed. The sunlight slanted across the green floor, and sounds of the bazaar came faintly through the open windows. Considering that the room contained ten children the stillness of it had a stealthy quality. Now and again there was an odd little whimper from a child, and Belinda babbled a strange lilting little tune to herself. Had

Belinda been heard and not seen one would have imagined her a contented twelve-month-old baby. She was fourteen, her face thin and ancient; her frail arms had the thinness of sticks and her curly hair was dry and lifeless. However, she smiled, waved her thin arms above the bed and babbled this endless melody to herself.

The eldest boy, aged twelve, suddenly started to slap himself violently in the face, round his eyes and nose, shouting loudly at the same time. He was unable to stop, and gradually his shouts turned to distressed tears because he was bruising himself. I held his hands to soothe him and he slowly quietened and went into a doze. But shortly afterwards he awoke and again began slapping himself; this time his shouts were so loud that the nurse from the opposite ward came in. She lifted him slightly from his pillows and cuddled him to her for a while, and put a soft teddy bear on his pillow. He again quietened down and slept.

At 4.10 I was still on my own in Blue Ward; the children were passive and quiet, some lying with their arms placed over the sheets and not moving at all, although they were awake. Matthew, the youngest child, aged three and with a kidney disease as well as mental subnormality, slept most of the time.

Lu-Lu played with her knitted doll tied on to her cot bars; she clenched her hand over its feet and pulled its plaited wool hair. Standing by Lu-Lu's cot I leant over and talked to her and pointed out to her the eyes and mouth of the doll; she copied my actions and a beautiful smile transformed her face. Lu-Lu responded more than most of the other children in Blue Ward. She would keep looking across the ward through her cot bars, and seemed to be attracting our attention; she longed for people to stand by her cot and talk to her; if nobody paid any attention to her glances she would become sad and large tears would roll down her thin face.

About 4.15 Matthew's parents came and woke him up to take him for a little walk. And, a little while afterwards, Freda's mother came to take her home for the night, apologizing to Freda for being so late. Freda got very excited, waved her arms up and down in a frenzy and made 'aaahh' noises.

'You'll sit up now,' said Freda's mother. 'You'll sit up now. Lie down all the week, and sit up on Sundays and Saturdays, eh?' She told me that they had a kitten at home and Freda loved it, and when she was at home the kitten would go to sleep in her arms. 'Yes, your kitty is waiting at home for you,' she said to Freda. Freda had been in the hospital for only a few weeks and her home contact was regular.

The afternoon continued quietly again after the parents went. One or two children whimpered and several heaved themselves slightly up so that they peered over the side of their beds or through their cot bars.

About 4.30 Matthew's parents brought him back from his walk, changed his nightdress and put him back in the cot. His mother walked around the ward and peeped into the other cots and beds. She was young and serious looking. 'It's pitiful,' she said. 'It's pitiful, I never knew, I never even guessed there were children like this until I brought my own child here when he got so ill, I'd no idea.' This mother regularly visited, and it was obvious that she deeply loved little Matthew. He was terribly frail and hopelessly brain-damaged and his little skull was slightly misshapen; he took ages to swallow any food and fretfully cried or dozed most of the time.

'We nearly lost him last year,' Matthew's mother went on. 'But they worked so hard for him and managed to save him. We really thought we'd lost him, but they were marvellous, absolutely marvellous. He was in a tent and everything, but they got him over it all.'

About 4.40 the nurse who was working in Blue Ward with me came back and said that it was time we started the feeding again. We began feeding at 5 o'clock. The nurse's teenage daughter and her two friends who had been to the bazaar came up into Blue Ward and helped us to feed, because we were a little late and there was a lot to do. The children could have either toasted cheese or tart and custard. Several of the children were not at all hungry and did not eat much, but they all enjoyed their drinks of tea afterwards.

With Freda having gone home there were only nine children to feed and with the three extra helpers we managed to finish by 6 o'clock. The three teenagers then went home and the nurse and I started to wash and change the children again. We shared the one hair-brush once more, and helped ourselves to clean nighties and nappies from the trolley as we needed them, and changed the sheets if necessary. We finished at 7 o'clock.

The last job was to clean the children's teeth. The nurse explained that we didn't have toothbrushes for the children. Instead, we put toothpaste on a piece of rag and rubbed their teeth with that and then wiped them dry with another piece of rag. Some of the children's teeth were mere black stumps and cleaning them like this was not pleasant. The nurse said that some of the parents didn't like the idea of their children not having toothbrushes, but she agreed with the hospital idea that toothbrushes were not very hygienic really, they only 'collected dust and got mixed up and everything'.

Between 7 and 7.30 we tidied round the ward, washed the washing-bowls and dried them, and tidied the linen. Other nurses sorted out dirty linen on the landing and stacked it ready to go down in the lift to the laundry. At 7.30 we all went off duty.

*

All through the day we had chatted as we worked; the nurses said they wondered what kept them going sometimes, they 'got that tired, and if you really thought about it all it was ever so depressing'.

'I like to be very quiet when I first get in of a night,' said an older nurse. 'I can't bear my husband to speak to me, just for a while you know, can't bear the kids to make a noise around me, sometimes I just go and get in the bath. But when I've had a bit to eat and drink then I'm all right again.'

'It makes you hard, this job does, it changes you, you know. It does, it makes you hard. No, not hard to the children, I'd never do anything to harm *them*, but it makes you sort of *different*. I don't know how, but just sort of *different*, it does something to you, changes you. When I first came, people said, everybody said, "You won't stick *that* for long," then, here I am, nine years later, still at it.' She laughed. 'Nine years, same thing, every day, same old things, feeding, changing, feeding, changing, makes you wonder. I've watched some of these children grow up. Same old routine, never varies.'

'People outside have no idea, they don't know about these poor little blighters, they don't care neither. But why *should* they care, after all, it's nothing to them?'

'I had a miscarriage once,' said another nurse. 'I was upset when it happened, awfully upset, but since then I've been here and seen these children and I've thought about it. I've thought. My baby might have been like these. In that case it was better to have lost him.'

'When I look at my own little girl, running around at home, I just can't believe that children can *be* like these.'

'I don't think I could leave a child of mine in hospital, however bad,' a young nurse said firmly; she had come into Blue Ward to fetch plates, and overheard.

'Oh, yes, I would, I know I would,' another nurse replied. 'I couldn't help it. Think how a child like this could ruin your family, ruin your life. If there were other children, too, you couldn't go anywhere, couldn't take the others on holiday, couldn't have people in, maybe.'

'It depends. It depends on if you have other children, where you live, depends on lots of other things.'

'Yes, it does, you can't *blame* anybody for what they decide to do, though.'

'That child there, Lu-Lu, her mum doesn't come to see her, doesn't want anything to do with her. You know what she said? "Leave her body to medical research when she dies." Did you ever hear anything so cruel, your own little girl, what a thing to say. That's wicked you know, to say that. She's beautiful, too. Aren't you beautiful, Lu-Lu?'

'You *are* beautiful, aren't you, love,' the nurses looked down over the cot sides at Lu-Lu and nodded to her, and she smiled back and excitedly shook her doll towards us.

'You know, if any of these kids gets ill, we fight for them, we really do. Put them in tents, bring them round. Again and again we think they're going and then we get them better. We really *fight* for them. We nearly lost young Matthew about three times. *And* Lu-Lu. She's not strong, you know. Very chesty in the winter. But we get them round again.'

Sunday

At 7.30 a.m. we started working again. I was on Blue Ward once more, but had a different nurse with me. We began by getting the trolley into the ward and starting to wash the children; they seemed to be lying in the same positions as when we had left them the previous evening. The nurse with me, middle-aged and with a family of her own, had worked several years in the wards of this building, and was a close friend of the nurse who had worked in Blue Ward on Saturday. She had brought her transistor radio with her and turned on the Light Programme; we listened to the music while we washed and changed the children.

I began with Jeff, aged eight; he was blind as well as totally physically handicapped and severely subnormal. He was very nice-looking, with a round well-shaped face and a clear complexion with just a sprinkling of freckles over his nose. Jeff was very dirty and needed clean nappies, draw sheet and nightdress. All the children wore the same type of nightdress, they were open at the back and fastened with three buttons in the front. They were yellow, blue and pink, much faded with all the laundering they went through.

At 8 o'clock the nurse went to see about getting the breakfasts, and we started feeding at 8.10. It took us until 9.30 to feed the nine children; we were helped by a junior nurse and the sister of the building. As the children finished breakfast we gave them each a drink of tea, which they enjoyed very much.

At 9.30 we started washing and changing the children again. There were seven children to do, as we had only managed to get Jeff and one other child changed before breakfast. We listened to the radio as we worked, and chatted to each other, sorting out dirty nappies and nightdresses as we went and putting them into the appropriate containers.

Again we used the thick paper napkins to wash the children. Having finished my first little girl I hunted round for the ward hairbrush but could not find it. The nurse said it must have gone into another ward. There was a large green comb on the trolley, but my little girl's hair was so matted that the comb would have been useless; so I did not do her hair at all, nor any other child's hair in Blue Ward that day.

At 9.45 the nurse went for her coffee break and I continued washing the children on my own. It was quiet in the ward, except for the Light Programme music and some occasional whimpers from the children. They seemed to like the continuous music. At 10 o'clock the nurse returned and it was my break-time.

When I got back to Blue Ward at 10.15 the nurse grimaced and said: 'You're going to love it up here later, all the kids except one have got to have suppositories.' We carried on washing and changing the children, changing bed linen and listening to the radio. Then a senior nurse came and gave out medicines to the children if they needed them, and the ward nurse gave the children the suppositories.

It was 11.30 when we finished all the washing and changing. Then we wiped the bowls out with a paper tissue and tidied up the trolley. We had time to relax then, and nurses from other wards came up to Blue Ward to listen to the radio and chat. We stood round Lu-Lu's cot, shaking her doll at her to make her smile, and the nurses discussed the bazaar.

Just before 12 o'clock the nurses went to see about getting the dinners up, and the routine of feeding began once more. The clean bibs were placed under the children's chins and we spooned meat, mashed potato and carrot to them. The nurse with me said that she did not 'get on' with fourteen-year-old Belinda, the child who babbled the endless little melody to herself.

'No, we don't like each other, we definitely don't,' the nurse explained. 'She doesn't like me and I don't like her. We both know it and respect each other, don't we, old girl?'

Belinda did not like being fed by this nurse and she continually spat food back at her. The nurse threatened Belinda that she would go without if she did not behave. Gradually Belinda swallowed some food, but she looked angry, waved her gaunt arms and made fretful noises of protest.

My lunch period was from 12.30 until 1.15. Then it was time to feed puddings whilst the other nurse went for her lunch period from 1.15 until 2 o'clock.

Having finished giving the puddings of mashed-up apple crumble and custard, I started the routine of washing and changing once more. Many of the children's nappies were badly soiled by now, which meant plenty of washing and changing of sheets, nappies and nighties. The smell in the ward began to get so dreadful that the windows had to be opened wide down each side. When the nurse came back from her lunch she hastily sprayed the room with an airspray in an attempt to freshen it up. We gradually grew accustomed to the smell as we worked continually with it, but if other nurses looked into the ward to speak to us they made horrified exclamations and laughed sympathetically.

We carried on washing and changing sheets, nighties and nappies, until 3.30. During this time a senior nurse again came round and gave out more drugs. We also gave some of the children drinks if they wanted them.

At 3.30 a mother came to visit one of the older girls, bringing a younger daughter with her. The little girl and the mother stood by the big girl's bed and the mother asked: 'Come for a walk? You'd like a walk, wouldn't you, dear?'

The little sister, aged about seven, solemnly stared as her mother dressed her big sister, in dress and underclothes, tights and shoes. The mother then lifted her helpless daughter over her shoulder in fireman fashion and carried her out on to the landing to go down in the lift to find a wheel-chair. They would take her for a walk in the park.

'She's amazing, that mum,' said the nurse, with admiration. 'Amazing, I call it. She's so nice, and she lifts that great girl up and carries her out. And she's always so cheerful and pleasant.'

After 3.30 we were relaxed again and talked to one or two nurses from other wards while we tidied up some linen and cleaned out the washing-bowls. At 4.15 I went for tea-break and returned to the ward at 4.30. We sat and chatted and listened to the radio.

At 5 o'clock we started the feeding routine again. The girl who had been for a push round the park with her mother and little sister returned to the ward, and her mother undressed her and put her to bed again. Before she went home this mother went and looked over the side of Lu-Lu's cot and watched her patting her knitted doll.

Then the little boy who had been home for a whole week-end was brought back into the ward by his mother and father and they undressed him and put him in his cot.

Feeding the children their supper took us until just after 6 o'clock; we were helped by an extra nurse and the sister of the building. Then we started the final washing routine of the day, changing nappies, washing bottoms and putting clean nighties on once more, and changing bed linen as necessary.

Freda, the little girl who had stayed away for Saturday night, was brought back at 6 o'clock. Her mother said that they had all had a happy week-end and Freda had loved seeing her kitten again. She quietly undressed Freda and put her back into her cot. Freda wept when her mother left, large tears rolling down her small round face.

During that week-end four of the children out of the eleven in Blue Ward had received family contact. Two had gone home to stay, and two had been taken for a little walk in the nearby park. Three of these four were younger children, aged under six. It seems that the older the severely subnormal children become the more tenuous is the hold they have on their families.

By about 7.10 we had finished doing the beds, changing nappies, and so on. Then we gave the ward a final tidy-up, washed the bowls, and put the soiled linen into the bags on the landing.

Nobody mentioned teeth-cleaning that evening. Maybe it was done by the night-staff. At 7.30 we went off duty.

Why and How do the Nurses Manage to Continue Doing this Work?

The married nurses were quite honest and said that they did it for the money and for convenience; they lived near and they managed to fit in the hours and days with their families. But in spite of this casual honesty that they liked the money, the nurses were not callous. They said that the work made them 'hard', but I saw no lack of genuine compassion. The help they gave the children in Blue Ward was good-hearted and practical; they did everything necessary for the physical well-being of the children, and worked hard to keep them warm, dry and well-fed, fulfilling the monotonous ward tasks almost jovially and with an easy comradeship with each other.

The fact that the nurses had homes and children of their own must have been a saving grace. To work with Blue Ward children in the mass for long periods would be a terrible strain for anybody who did not have an ordinary family life to go back to each night.

The nurses were well aware that the Blue Ward children had irreversible brain damage and that their conditions were hopeless. All their working hours the nurses contended with meaningless fretful squeals and whimpers, the ceaseless writhings of uncontrolled limbs, the self-hitting of the big twelve-year-old boy, the drawing up and crossing of legs which is typical of cerebral palsied children and which makes nappie changing so difficult; they contended daily with frequent and unpleasant smells.

Sometimes the room would be filled with a medley of cries and fretful whimpers that would rise to a crescendo of distress; at other times the room would be sombrely quiet, a quiet made less easy by the knowledge that ten children were present.

There was the endless repetition of the same routine, changing nappies, changing nighties, changing sheets, washing faces and bodies, spooning pap food into jaws that were so uncontrollable that sometimes they opened too wide or sometimes not at all.

Thus the nurses passed their working hours.

Our veneration of the basic fact of being physically alive, a veneration that weirdly contradicts our humane responsibilities and results in magnificent efforts to maintain the existence of such sad travesties of human life, confuses one when confronted with these severely subnormal children in the mass.

These words 'in the mass' are the operative words upon which would hinge any criticisms that might be made about the living conditions for these children. Why on earth are they ever kept in large groups like this? How is it that society can be so short-sighted that it permits children with total handicaps of this serious nature to be herded together? Hospitals containing many seriously subnormal children all together are nothing more than compounds of distress; they should never be kept in large numbers all under one roof.

Would it not be wiser and more humane, although terribly difficult to organize in its initial stages, if a plan was made to distribute our seriously subnormal children in small numbers to residential homes and schools, hostels, ordinary hospitals, or old people's Homes and residential nursery schools? In the same way as the blind or physically disabled are absorbed into industry – the car industry employs a percentage of disabled – so surely could one or two seriously subnormal children be tolerated and absorbed into groups of more able children. They would learn a little from a more stimulating environment and way of life, and the other people around them might even gain in tolerance and understanding by having them there.

From personal experience I maintain that such an arrangement could be made to work if the numbers were kept to only one or two. For in my own nursery class of physically handicapped children there has always been included over the last five years a girl who is no better off intellectually than the children on Blue Ward. Each day this child, now aged ten, is dressed, put into her wheel-chair and brought to nursery school. She sees life from an upright position, she enjoys being in school and listens to what goes on. Her smile is content and her interest in the day is alert, despite her severe mental disability. She has been able to make the most of what limited responses she has. Compared to the children like her in Blue Ward, she is most fortunate and does not feel that she has missed out on opportunities that she should have. Whereas any small percentage of intelligence that the seriously subnormal children of Blue Ward had would surely be entirely crushed by the poverty of their existence in the one large group in that ward?

What About Lu-Lu?

Lu-Lu grabbed at her cup when she was being helped with a drink.

'Look,' called a young nurse standing by her cot. 'She wants to hold her cup herself. She tries, she does. Can she have a spoon to hold?'

'Yes, give her a spoon,' replied the older nurse. 'She'll like that.'

Lu-Lu was given a spoon; lying in her cot she banged the spoon against the bars and smiled her sweet smile as three of us stood looking down over the cot rail at her. She suddenly saw that her plastic cup had fallen between the cot sides and mattress; she grasped it in her hand and held it up to us.

'Ah, I'm sure she's got more in her than some of the others here,' somebody murmured.

Later on, as I was washing Lu-Lu, she clutched the towel from where I had put it over the top rail of her cot. I was busy soaping the paper tissue to wash her feet and when I turned again to her I was surprised to see her rubbing the towel up and down as she tried to dry her thin chest. Watching her pathetic attempts to dry her own helpless body, I wondered. Grossly handicapped children like Lu-Lu are not unfamiliar to me; when we work with badly handicapped children we try (foolishly perhaps) to see greater intelligence in them than they might possibly possess; but what *about* Lu-Lu? What if she did have more ability than people realized? Exiled from normality in the dull bed-ridden existence afforded in Blue Ward, virtually abandoned by her mother, any potential ability that Lu-Lu might have would eventually evanesce.

When I had finished washing Lu-Lu I sat her cross-legged at the end of her cot whilst I tidied her pillows. She grasped the metal frame of her bed cradle in one hand and banged it with the spoon she held in her other hand.

'She is all right to sit cross-legged, isn't she?' I checked with the nurse.

'Yes, it will do her good.'

Lu-Lu's ready smile appeared. For a moment she was seeing her world from a different angle. She held her head a little more upright; her dark eyes alight with an almost mischievous triumph, she grinned broadly.

What Does Hospitalization Do to Children?

The diaries of the children's week-ends speak for themselves, and we need not look beyond them to establish that children in hospital can suffer deprivation. But what does hospitalization actually do to the children? How do the children show the effects of their deprivation? It is possible that nobody yet knows, or ever will know, the exact and long-term effects on the children, but there are some effects which are apparent to even the most casual observer and are seen in the children's play patterns, their language and conversation, their relationships with other people and each other, their demands for attention and their poor socialization.

Play

The play of the Fieldway School children followed a pattern which was fairly typical of children with mental and physical disabilities, being similar to children without handicaps, but lacking in maturity and originality. But the children in Ridge Hospital displayed play characteristics which were not usually found amongst children in residential schools. One characteristic was the *suddenness of their play*, the tendency for short, quick, utter involvement in something; for example, a child would momentarily get a toy – a policeman's helmet, or false teeth – and he would play intensely and almost hysterically with the object for just a few moments, laughing, and hurrying up and down with it. Then he would just as suddenly abandon the object and completely lose interest in it.

Another characteristic was the *plea for a grown-up to perform the play activity*. The children would say:

'Will *you* colour this picture?'
'Will *you* do this cutting out?'
'*You* can join up these dots.'

Even when the child was physically capable and intelligent enough to handle the scissors and material he would still make this request. It was as if the *getting of an adult to join in with something close to him* was more important to the child than the actual occupation itself. The children in the schools would take the pencil or the scissors and say: 'I can do it, give it to me.' Then they would proudly show the finished article. But for the hospital child the finished object was less important than the primary power it had possessed in bringing an adult near and in contact with him; it was often noticed that if the adult moved away then the child completely lost interest in the activity and, when it was finished, he soon discarded it.

The hospital child sometimes took little notice of the colouring or cutting out whilst the adult was doing it; he would perhaps look rather blankly elsewhere, but if the adult decided the activity was finished and made to move away, then the child would quickly say: 'Don't go, do some more, you haven't finished.'

It was curious to find that a child who was new to Fieldway School, but whom I had known previously in a long-term hospital, still showed this characteristic behaviour, which she had displayed excessively during her long stay in the hospital. Even in the security of the school she still craved for an adult to be involved in her play and the adult's attention was more important than the play. However, over a period of six months visiting the school, this play pattern was seen to be lessening. Did it lessen because of the security she found in her new school and the permanence of a housemother? Was it originally caused by the insecurity of the hospital because of their constantly changing staff, and the child's inability to get a grown-up to stay with her, and her need to find a mother?

Another play characteristic was the *holding of objects and toys rather than actively playing* with them. This was very noticeable amongst the children in Ridge Hospital. The children in the two Schools played constructively with objects, they *built* with bricks, *pushed* trucks along, *built* a blanket house, pretended to *sell* petrol, *operated* on their dolls. But the hospital children did not play constructively or with imagination; children in Ridge Hospital were noticed just holding an empty talcum powder tin as they sat at their tables, or they sat with an unopened book in front of them, or they passively kept their hand over a toy. This holding habit may have been partly due to lack of stimulation from the staff, and partly because the wards were grouped according to ages which meant that the children did not mix with others at various stages of development who might have stimulated a variety of ideas.

The holding habit might also have been caused by the crowded conditions of the wards, which meant that, if they let go, then the precious possession could be snatched from them and lost for ever in the general muddle of the ward; or it may have been that they just derived some vague comfort through having something to hang on to in all the confusion of their enclosed little world. Another characteristic of the children in Ridge Hospital was their inability to play in groups. The children aged between six and ten were of an age when it would have been normal for them to play happily in groups, but they showed no desire to do so, and just seemed to be intensely irritated by each other most of the time. The inability to play in groups might have been due to a lack of toys, the hours spent in functional routines (getting toileted sometimes took three or four hours every day), the overcrowded living conditions, and the lack of staff guidance in activities.

Another characteristic of hospital children's play was playing at pricks, plasters and operations. This was most evident amongst the youngest children at Ridge; it was also seen amongst the Larchdale School children who had undergone surgical treatments. I saw children sitting down waiting for meals, or sitting in front of the television set who would roll each other's sleeves up and pretend to give pricks with needles, or would say:

'I will plaster your arm.'

'Your arm has to be plastered.'

The child having the prick or plaster would be very submissive and when the other child had finished he would pretend to cry and then say:

'Now, I'll give *you* a prick.'

Sometimes visitors would also be told that they would have to have pricks and operations.

It is obvious that this form of play, which was a fairly normal re-creation of a situation in which a child had something nasty done to him, stemmed directly from the hospital environment, being based sometimes on the child's own experiences and sometimes on things which he had watched being done to other children although he himself would not have any hospital treatments.

A *lack of play initiative* was typical of the children in Ridge Hospital; they would sometimes just stand still, or sit staring for twenty minutes at a time. Children often just walked up and down, perhaps aimlessly opening and closing locker doors as they went. They would sometimes say: 'What *can* we do?' Then, one of them would suggest in a very bright voice: 'Shall we tidy the lockers?'

Age-segregation may have been administratively convenient, but it was unnatural for the children, and may have been one of the causes of retarded play initiative. Children learn through experiencing normal family and neighbourhood situations and witnessing the play of variously aged children; but children who live in hospital, segregated into their own age-group, lack these stimulating learning experiences. When all four- and five-year-old children are kept together, they experience only the naturally tempestuous behaviour of the young child.

Age-segregation retards not only the child's play development, but also his social development. When older children are not in contact with younger ones they miss the experience of 'mothering'. In the residential schools the younger children saw the older ones helping at meals and it was expected that they helped with the younger and more helpless ones. Older children taught the younger ones how to play cards, how to knit and dress their dolls.

Another aspect of age-segregation was that when a child was moved to another ward because he reached a certain age, then it was quite likely that he never again had a chance to meet the children from his old ward with whom he had perhaps lived for several years. There was no encouragement to visit each other's ward, they never went 'out to tea' or 'out to play' with each other as children normally do in a neighbourhood situation.

Language and Conversation

The schoolchildren's conversation was not always very rich, for some of them were mentally limited, but it was lively and varied, and showed individual interests. Fieldway School children talked about the pictures in the bedrooms, the flowers growing up the drive, the dead bird, the bonfire, the lamb and how he should be looked after. They had plenty of childish interests and experiences, and could communicate with other people in an outward-looking manner and not merely in terms of their own handicaps or environment. Even a very deaf girl in Fieldway managed to ask me:

'Did you knit your own jumper, it is nice?'
'Where is your car?'
'Where is your house?'

The conversation of the long-stay hospital children was of a poor quality, more often than not being limited to affairs of the ward and the duties of the staff.

'Are you on at biggend?'
'Do you come from littlend?'
'Who is on *next*?'
'What time are you off?'
'Who is on tomorrow?'
'When is sister on?'
'Are you going off now?'
'Who will be on tonight?'

And as they rested on their beds the children talked about pricks, bandages, plasters and operations.

'Do you know Betty has a patch on her tummy?'
'Sister has to do the patch.'
'Have you got a pain in you tummy? If I get a pain in my tummy I shall have to go to the hostable.'
'Shall I sent my mummy to hostable?'

The children were also liable suddenly to push up a visitor's sleeve, if they were standing near, and say in loud authoritarian voices: 'Now, you must have your prick, keep still, you naughty girl.'

The children at Ridge had curious, almost adult, habits of discussing their bodily functions, which was typical of hospital living. One six-year-old girl, who was handicapped by thalidomide, asked me to take her to the toilet. As she explained the procedure for toileting her and how to work the sluice afterwards, she said: 'You are *learning*, aren't you? Now you know how to do *me*. If you come again, I will show you again in case you forget. I always show people who are learning. You have to learn.'

Some of the children even asked if I was their mummy. This came from children who rarely had visitors from home, and no regular or recent contact with their mothers. They just thought that a 'mummy' was a lady who was not in nurse's uniform and who turned up to make a special fuss of certain lucky children. They lived in hope that the next stranger who appeared in the ward would turn out to be their own 'mummy', so they would hurry over, or call out frantically and ask the important question so they could establish their claim as soon as possible.

The poverty of the conversation in Ridge Hospital was partly caused by the children having very little verbal contact with the staff, who always seemed to be too busy to stop and talk. This lack of time to talk to the children was not found in the schools, where it was common to see houseparents and nurses sitting down and talking to children and encouraging them to chat; the staff would stop and listen carefully to what a child was trying to say, even if he had a speech defect and was slow to make himself understood.

In Ridge Hospital, however, the nurses rarely sat down and talked to the children, because their performance of duties took all their time. On one occasion, a child who was ready for the night and in her cot called out to the staff nurse who was getting other children ready for bed. This staff nurse was too busy to stop and see what the child wanted, so the little girl began to call rhythmically 'Staff, staff'. Then she chanted for long minutes, without stopping: 'Tarf, ta-arf, ta-arf, ta-arf.' Finally she lapsed into a chant of 'Darf-darf, darf-darf, darf-darf', nodding her head and rocking at the same time. Nobody went to her, and this chanting continued for fifteen minutes, only stopping when the evening drinks were brought round. The nurses did not refer to her pleas for attention or ask her what she wanted when they gave her her drink.

In a strange, frightening or crowded situation a child's only means of reassurance is to have one adult or mother-substitute of his own. If, as on the wards, this is not possible, then he needs reassurance from the many adults who pass daily through his life. Even if it means the constant answering of repetitive, seemingly unnecessary, questions, and time-consuming explanations, an effort should be made to give this reassurance. However, this did not happen in the hospital.

Mealtimes can often be a time of sociable conversation and an opportunity for learning something. In the schools the children were encouraged to talk about the food, and the staff would ask:

'What are those nuts called?'

'Do you like beans?'

'Where did this egg come from? Can you remember the name of the place?'

At Ridge the staff talked a lot about table-manners in an authoritarian and not very helpful way. They would say:

'Now, come on, eat properly, hurry up now.'

'Don't drink like that.'

'Look at all that mess you've made.'

Between 1.15 and 2 o'clock was a time when conversation could have been made at Ridge, for then the children were just sitting around in the ward, nobody was having to be 'done' in the lavatory, and no meals were being served. However, the children *remained just sitting silently*, whilst the nurses moved around the ward polishing the piano, wiping lockers and wiping tables with disinfectant cloths. They did not speak to the children during this period.

On the Sunday at Ridge, there were only two examples of real conversation taking place. (This was observed throughout a period from 7.50 a.m. until 7 p.m. with just two fifteen-minute periods away from the ward.) These two episodes of conversation both concerned the same senior nurse. A boy of six wanted to get in the linen cupboard, on to the shelf marked with his name, and the nurse let him do this and he sat in there, grinning broadly; then he had five minutes' chat with the nurse, which she encouraged, all about the size of the shelf and the letters of the names on the other shelves. Later on, this nurse talked to another little boy, aged five, who badly wanted to wear his toy watch in bed at night; the nurse persuaded him to leave it off, explaining carefully how she took her own watch off every night; this took about ten minutes, and the little boy listened seriously.

It is significant that this nurse was a senior member of staff, and had some personal responsibility towards the children and her own decisions about them, unlike the junior nurses who were always under pressure to get on with their duties and appeared loath to take even a simple decision such as playing with a child. Proof that it is the pressure of duties which does a lot to prevent personal contact with the children is supported by the fact that one evening a nurse missed her bus into town, so she came back when off duty to help put the children to bed. She was relaxed, with no pressure of duties, as she was officially 'off'. She took children on to her lap, chatted to them and gave them a lot of attention.

Changes of staff can encourage lack of verbal contact, for there are always fairly new, or completely new, nurses learning the ward procedures. Sometimes, too, there are language problems caused by overseas girls who have taken hospital jobs for a temporary period in order to learn English. For example, one overseas night-nurse got all the children out of their cots one morning without speaking to them.

The children's lack of personal conversation had effects on their behaviour in other ways; for example, there was a lot of shouting in strained high-pitched voices at Ridge; there was also habitual rhythmic calling of staff, without any real expectation of receiving a reply; and amongst the older children there was an intense craving for conversation, as when Tony said, 'Come and talk to me. Can we just *talk*? Sit and talk to me. Just talk. Talk about something to me, that's what I like doing best of all.'

The growth of language, and verbal contact between adult and child and between child and child, are two of the most important aspects of child development. It is possible that, next to loss of mother, the most serious result of hospitalizing a child is his lack of verbal contact with the adults who care for him. One can describe this lack of verbal contact as 'lingual deprivation'; it has been noticed in many hospitals and appears typical of institutionalization.

Relationships with Each Other and Other People

Unlike the children in the schools, whose relationships with each other were uncomplicated and friendly, with an occasional fight and argument, the long-stay Ridge Hospital children seemed unhappy with each other and had poor relationships. There was constant squabbling and scrapping; some of the scrapping could be accepted as usual behaviour, but it was often too prolonged and distressing for normality. Most of the bickering took place without any preliminary argument or conversation and consisted of near-silent pushing, pulling, slapping or snatching, and it inevitably ended in screams and cries. The children also seemed very irritated by each other. A child would often have one of his belongings snatched by another child, who would then make off down the ward, throwing it over his shoulder as he went, or discarding it just out of reach of the child to whom it belonged. This sort of behaviour went on continually. There was also an overall reluctance to share belongings, and pencils and books were sometimes hidden away so that other children could not find them and use them.

There was a lot of jealousy amongst the children about which of them had my attention when I was talking to them. On several occasions the children who had sat on my lap were pushed, pinched and slapped afterwards. On the other hand, there were some intense, almost emotional friendships, which consisted of the children cuddling and kissing each other. When nursery-ward children were together in prams they kissed and cuddled each other as they were pushed along. And a child who had recently returned to the ward after having been away to have an operation in another hospital was made a tremendous fuss of; the other children begged to be allowed to sit near her, they patted and stroked her as she ate her meals. Some children who could not get near her cried and asked to be lifted over. She was overwhelmed with patting and fondling and eventually the sister had to tell the children to leave her alone.

A similar pattern of behaviour was noticed with regard to a smaller child who had a very dominant personality. The other children used to ask if he could sit on their cots after they were ready for bed. Although not very much younger, this child was much smaller than the rest of the children; they would take turns to have him on their beds and were very tender in their care of him, and would hold a book up for him to see.

At other times the children appeared very callous to each other at Ridge, and quite indifferent to witnessing scenes of distress. A child would sometimes sit, holding a toy, absorbed and quite unperturbed, completely ignoring other children beside him who would be crying inconsolably because they had dropped things and nobody would pick them up. It seemed as if their relationships vacillated between anxious 'caring' for each other and extreme callousness; there were none of the moderate childish friendships such as were found in the schools.

Was it possible that, because the long-stay Ridge Hospital children were deprived of a family or affectionate mother-substitutes, their relationships with each other took on the emotional overtones of mother–child relationships, viz. their patting, kissing and cuddling; this relationship was at the same time confused by the irritations caused by their overcrowding and the affection they craved from the adults.

The fact that the children were unable to be alone affected their relationships. Lacking solitude and quiet, they risked being exhausted by noise, and the excessive proximity one to another caused distress, anxiety, excitement and quarrels; these highly strung reactions were not seen in the more spacious environment of the schools. It was glaringly obvious that more space and rooms were needed in long-stay hospitals.

It is obvious that group relationships will be influenced by the organization of the hospital. When children spend their whole childhood in hospital, and are segregated by ages, as happened in Ridge Hospital, then the children are denied practice in forming satisfactory relationships, an experience which would be

Children in Hospitals 147

normal to them if living in a family and neighbourhood. Children need to mix with various ages in order to learn their social behaviour.

Another reason for the children's disunity in Ridge Hospital may have been the authoritarian and constantly changing staff. A situation in which the staff are authoritarian and constantly changing and have to care for a group of children all of the same age and all living in one room does not encourage the formation of good relationships. Each child in such a group will remain in a void, gaining nothing from the others and giving nothing in return; he will tend to quarrel, be suspicious and unfriendly, fearful, timid, isolated although in a crowd, excessively demanding from any adult who will pay him attention, jealous, and forming only very shallow relationships.

The children's attitudes towards the staff varied in the different places. For example, in Fieldway School the children's attitudes seemed to be influenced by their severe physical handicaps, their mental limitations and their family deprivations; they relied on the staff for affection and mothering. Although the children were encouraged to be independent – they cared for themselves as much as they could – washing, feeding and dressing, they nevertheless relied on the houseparents for decisions about going for walks, organizing games, choosing television programmes and so on.

The children at Larchdale School were very independent and did not demand so much mothering and affection from the staff. Although they were badly handicapped physically, and needed the practical assistance of the staff, there was an air of almost jaunty self-reliance which was a little unusual amongst a group of handicapped children. One reason for their independence may have been the fact that they were not mentally limited, nor so multiply handicapped as the Fieldway School children, for none of them needed feeding and all of them could speak and sit up straight. Also, the Larchdale children nearly all came from families which maintained good contact with them, which meant that they did not have to depend solely on houseparents for affection.

The child-staff relationships in Ridge Hospital were very negative and there was little attempt to make close relationships. The reasons for this negative attitude may have been due to the lack of training in child care, the quick change-over of staff, the language barrier of the overseas staff, the authoritarian attitudes of the staff in charge, the children's lack of family contact and their extremely long stays in the hospital. All these factors had a depressive effect on personal relationships.

Demands for Attention

Demanding attention is a typical behaviour problem associated with children who live in institutions and are cared for by many different people. Demands were excessive at Ridge Hospital and only very slight in the schools. At Fieldway School the most stringent demands for attention came from children who had a history of earlier hospitalization or separation from their families through family breakdown or family rejection.

At Ridge Hospital, the children called out at the appearance of any stranger and rushed forward in their wheel-chairs. When I first arrived, although they had never seen me before, they all called out:

'Come *here*, lady.'
'Come here to *me*, lady.'
'Hello, hello, come here, lady.'

When a visitor was walking down the ward the children in chairs caught hold of their clothes and hands and tried to make them stay. They sometimes pressed their heads against a visitor's knee or arm, quite silently. When they played, they appeared not so much to want the adult to *play* with them but rather to *remain near*; the pleas to have help in crayoning and cutting-out were all too often just pathetic excuses to have a few minutes' individual attention. When eight- or nine-year-old children saw a younger child sitting on one's lap, they would sometimes come up in their wheel-chair and say: 'I'm too big to sit on your lap, aren't I?' Then, if they were confined to wheel-chairs, they would do the nearest thing they could towards getting on one's lap – they would lean out of the chair and just rest their head down on one's arm.

If a visitor came to one particular child, then other children would circle round and silently watch, hoping to obtain some little scrap of attention. They became wildly excited at the arrival of the hospital shop-trolley, but the things they bought were discarded very soon after it went. It was typical that the arrival of anything that would temporarily give them an adult's attention made them anxiously clamour.

If one did not satisfy the demands of the children they were liable to burst into frenzied tears, although this instant sobbing did not occur if they called the nurses and received no response. It seemed as if the children never *expected* to receive attention from the nurses in the form of cuddles and time on laps, but always hoped that this attention would be forthcoming from visitors or voluntary workers; then they suffered catastrophic disappointment if their expectations were not satisfied. This differentiation, between the ward staff who did not have time to give them affectionate attention, and the visitors or helpers who probably would, was an ominous characteristic of the smallest children at Ridge. It was similar to when they automatically named somebody who read them a story as 'teacher'. All too frequently, these children categorized adults into set roles, as nurses, teachers, sisters, mummies, students, visitors; then they expected them to behave strictly according to their role. A teacher's role was to provide interesting attention, books, paper and occupations; a nurse's role was to attend to functional needs, the meals, going to the lavatory and washing; sisters were in charge of treatment, and took decisions about pricks; mummies brought presents and made a fuss of you; in the narrow, hierarchy-influenced world of the hospital, children soon learned to label adults.

Socialization

'Socialization' refers to the skills, behaviour and attitudes which children acquire through their contact with other people: their family, relations, friends, teachers, neighbours; or, in relation to the children in this study, the people in their institutions. The quality of the socialization is reflected in the community's behaviour patterns, which, over a period of time, become characteristic of that particular community. Good socialization within an institution has characteristics which are acceptable to the world outside the institution. A few of these acceptable characteristics would be: kindness to others, amicable sharing of toys and possessions, an ability to wait contentedly for attention, table manners, taking part in household chores, good communication with each other and an enjoyment of independence.

It was obvious that good socialization was successfully taking place in the school institutions, for the children *were* kind to each other, they shared their toys, they were patient when waiting for attention, their table manners were as pleasant as their gross handicaps allowed, they helped with household chores, they had good communication with each other and enjoyed independence. In Ridge Hospital, however, there was a poor standard of socialization, and the characteristic behaviour patterns within that particular institution would have been unacceptable to the world outside, that is to an ordinary family, a School, or a Children's Home. If a young child has a prolonged stay in an institution which has a low standard of socialization, then he runs the risk of irreversible social maladjustment.

It appears, from the diaries and the subsequent discussion about the children's behaviour, that handicapped children who live in hospital are vulnerable to various forms of deprivation which may eventually create *additional handicaps* for them. These additional handicaps are further intellectual retardation, social incompetence and deep-seated unhappiness.

Part Three
People Who Work in Hospitals

Teachers

There are two categories of hospital teacher: first, those who teach the mentally disabled children who, until April 1971, came under the administration of the Ministry of Health for their education. These children are very handicapped intellectually and have previously been excluded from the educational services given by the DES, not even being officially permitted to have Special Education (although there are some seriously subnormal children unofficially accepted in Special Schools). Before the 1959 Mental Health Act these children would have been described as idiots and imbeciles, but they are now called 'severely subnormal'; their I.Q. is generally well below 50. In 1971 the administration of their education was transferred to the DES and they are now included in the LEA Special School services which are given to all the other categories of handicapped children. At present, some of their teachers are qualified under the Training Council for Teachers of the Mentally Handicapped or the National Association of Mental Health, some are Ministry of Education qualified teachers, some are without any qualifications at all. The unqualified teachers have sometimes had training in nursing, nursery nursing or residential child-care, which has given them experience with children, but the majority have had no experience with handicapped children and come from all kinds of jobs: secretaries, shop assistants, telephonists, domestic workers, hotel employees and housewives.

Hospitals for the mentally subnormal usually have a school on their premises if they accommodate any patients under sixteen. The school is sometimes in a ward, but often it is a purpose-built building in the grounds of the hospital. The children go to the school from their wards each day, attending for approximately the same number of hours as children in Ministry of Education schools. Those teachers who have any sort of qualification are usually in a position of responsibility in the school, being the Head or Deputy Head. They are offically described as 'supervisors', whilst their staff are described as 'assistants'. In 1968 there were 127 Supervisors and Assistants in hospital schools (for the Subnormal) who were qualified, and there were 489 Assistants who were unqualified.

Secondly, there are those teachers who have always come under the DES and teach in hospitals which cater for children whose main disability is a physical one, but which may include some retarded children. These hospital teachers are employed by Local Education Authorities, they are qualified according to the DES regulations for teachers in ordinary schools, they receive Burnham salaries plus Special School Allowances, and they have the same hours and holidays as teachers at LEA primary schools. The teaching may be done in the hospital wards, or in rooms adjoining the wards, or in a classroom block in the grounds. Sometimes the LEA pays 'rent' to the hospital for the use of a hospital building as a school. The children with whom these teachers work may be in hospital for just a few weeks, for a year or two, or for most of their childhood.

To avoid confusing the two categories of hospital teachers, in the following pages the teachers working in hospital schools for the severely subnormal children who came under the Ministry of Health until April 1971 will always be referred to as 'supervisors' or 'assistants' (regardless of their qualifications) whereas the teachers whose children have always been under the DES will be referred to throughout as 'teachers'.

The Role of the Teacher in Hospital Schools

Children in hospital schools will have a variety of chronic handicaps or acute illnesses, so the hospital teacher might be working with a group of children whom she will get to know thoroughly over the course of several years; or she might work with children in short-stay wards who do not stay in hospital more than a week or two; or, between these two extremes, with children who have some disorder which necessitates several months in hospital at a time and frequent re-admissions for further treatment.

Some hospital teaching is done at bedsides, and in short-stay wards there is often a very wide age range which might mean that the teacher has a small child in a cot at one end of the ward and an adolescent studying for A-levels at the other end. In the long-stay wards the children will not be in bed, they are up and dressed and in wheel-chairs or running about the ward. The long-stay children are usually grouped according to age, which is more convenient for teaching purposes.

Teaching in hospitals is a popular job and there are always plenty of applicants for every vacancy advertised. The salary is the same as for teachers in Day Special Schools, but there are the advantages of no playground duties, no dinner-duties (meals are the nurses' responsibility) and no dinner-money collecting. Some of the reasons given by teachers for wanting to teach in hospital have been that it is more exciting than ordinary school; that teachers wanted to mix with a wider staff, not just teachers, but a staff that includes doctors and nurses; that they had always had an interest in children's illnesses; that they wanted to do something useful; that ordinary school-teaching made them feel in a rut. Some chose it because they had had discipline troubles in secondary schools and thought it would be easier in a hospital, with the children in bed; some wanted to do something medical, but not nursing, and some simply wanted smaller classes.

Sometimes the applicants had visited a hospital during their training and this had interested them. A few teachers in hospitals have come from other Special Schools, but most of them have gone straight into hospital teaching from ordinary schools and have had no experience with handicapped children. After a period of several years' teaching in a hospital some teachers go on to do a year's course for a Diploma in the Education of Handicapped Children (or similar Diploma).

Teachers have a variety of complaints: too many visitors on the short-stay wards; parents in and out all day; the visitors never realize the children are supposed to be having school and they keep interrupting; the grans keep coming in and piling the children up with presents and sweets; interruptions by medical staff; the doctors are so haughty; the sisters are afraid that teachers will make a mess in their ward; sometimes the short-stay children all get discharged at once, so that there is nothing much to do all day; the long-stay children never get discharged and they are so dull that teaching them seems almost a waste of time.

On the other hand, satisfied teachers have said that the atmosphere was pleasant, the sister was pro-school; that it was better than the narrowness of ordinary school teaching; that it was bliss never to have dinner-duties; and that in small groups, you get to know the children.

Questions relating to hospital teaching were put to the staff of a large hospital school; there were twenty-eight on the school staff and fourteen consented to answer questions. The length of time that the fourteen teachers had worked in the hospital varied from one year up to twenty-one years. Seven had been there from one to three years, the other seven had been there more than ten years. The hospital took long-stay and short-stay children, with a variety of chronic handicaps and acute illnesses. On the same premises there was a school and wards for seriously subnormal children, but the teachers had nothing to do with that section of the hospital.

These are the answers of the seven teachers who had worked in the hospital from one to three years.

Have you had any training in teaching handicapped children, or in social work, or residential child care?

One teacher had a two-year certificate in nursery nursing. One had attended a short course of a few weeks' duration related to remedial reading, and a course lasting two weeks on the needs of autistic children. The other five had no special training related to handicapped children.

Do you organize any out-of-school activities for the children?

Three never organized any activities for the children to do after school. Two said that very occasionally they gave books to 'suitable children' to read for homework. The remaining two, who worked with autistic children, took the children to shops and sometimes home with them.

Do you leave school equipment out for children to use in out-of-school hours?

All seven answered no. The reasons they gave for not leaving anything out was that it would get lost, damaged, broken, 'destroyed by any subnormal children there might be on the ward'. All seven said that the school cupboards were kept locked when they were not there. One said that she thought the ward was adequately stocked with materials and that school equipment was not needed after school.

Would you be willing to do extraneous duties?

If so, would you prefer the duties to be part of the work expected of hospital teaching, and paid for by your LEA, or would you prefer it to be on a voluntary basis?

One teacher said she would definitely never consent to extra duties, paid or unpaid. The other six said 'perhaps occasionally' and 'if necessary', but they really wanted 'time to relax' and needed to 'follow their own leisure pursuits'. Of those six only one said that she would like the duties to be paid for and part of the expected work of a hospital teacher, and she added that she would want to stipulate herself exactly what she would do. The other five said the duties would have to be voluntary and arranged to fit in with their personal convenience.

Have you had any occasion to visit the ward during the week-end in the last twelve months, and if so, what were the children doing?

Five of the seven said that they had never visited the ward during any week-ends; two said that they had and the children had no occupations at all.

Do you think hospital staff might be interested in teachers organizing week-end activities for the children?

Two of the seven said no; the other five said that the nurses would probably be interested, especially if the children were long-stay and the parents did not visit.

What do you think of staggering school holidays so that the school is never closed?

Three of the seven teachers thought it would be a bad idea for short-stay children who were admitted to hospital during their own school holidays because it would mean that those children would not have a holiday. Three thought it would have a lot in its favour, but would need careful arranging so that it did not interfere with their personal commitments. One teacher thought that the nursing staff and children would like it, as holidays were always so empty, but that the teachers would have too many personal arguments against it.

Do you have regular ward/teaching staff meetings on your ward?

Only one of the seven said that there were weekly staff meetings between the nurses and teachers on her ward. The other six said there were never any meetings; and when asked about parent/teacher/ward staff meetings, all seven said there had never been meetings of that kind held at all.

Do you know any of the parents of your children?

Six of the teachers met them during visiting hours and knew most of them, but one teacher did not know any of the parents at all.

Would you be willing to have one or two (not more) seriously subnormal children in your group of physically disabled children?

Two teachers who worked with autistic children said that their children were considered in the category of seriously subnormal already. The other five teachers were definitely against such an idea; the reasons they put forward were: 'unfair on children working for exams'; 'it would disturb the others, not to mention any attempts by the teacher to give formal lessons'; 'one child like that could disrupt a whole group'; 'only if it did not seriously affect the average children'; 'tend to be disruptive and time-consuming'.

Do you think that hospital schools should send school reports home?

Six of the seven were in favour of this idea, but the seventh said, 'No, an interested parent asks about their child's progress when they visit generally, if they don't visit then they are not interested in the child anyway.'

These are the answers of the seven teachers who had worked in the hospital between ten and twenty-one years.

Have you had any training in teaching handicapped children, or in social work, or residential child care?

Five of the seven had had no special training at all; one had attended a six-week course within the hospital, on the manage-

People Who Work in Hospitals 159

ment of cerebral palsied children; one had attended a year's University course and obtained a certificate in teaching physically handicapped children. (When their years of service in that hospital were added up they totalled 110, with only one year and six weeks of special training between them.)

Do you organize any out-of-school activities for the children?

Three were most emphatic that they did not consider this to be part of their job (one saying that 'one needs to get away from children during out-of-school hours'). Three said that they gave their children occasional 'homework'. One had been responsible for organizing a music club which had met regularly for over ten years, once a fortnight after school in a building in the hospital grounds. Long-stay chronically handicapped children had attended the club.

Do you leave school equipment out for children to use in out-of-school hours?

All seven said it was kept locked up in the cupboards when they were not there. The reasons they gave for not leaving school equipment out were: 'would get lost and broken'; 'would soon be spoilt'; 'would lose importance as special school equipment'; 'lost too quickly by irresponsible nurses'; 'visiting times occupy the children most of the time and they usually have adequate equipment on the ward'; 'against school policy'; 'it belongs to the Education Authority'.

Would you be willing to do extraneous duties? If so, would you prefer the duties to be part of the work expected of hospital teaching, and paid for by your LEA, or would you prefer it to be on a voluntary basis?

Four of the seven said that perhaps they would be willing to do some form of extraneous duty as long as it fitted in with their own personal commitments, and was entirely voluntary. Three were strongly against the idea in any form.

Have you had any occasion to visit the ward during the weekend in the last twelve months, and if so, what were the children doing?

Four of the seven said they had been to the wards at a weekend, and they found the children playing, being visited, watching television, reading, sitting in the sun in the courtyards, making models (teenage boys), doing nothing. Three teachers had not visited and did not know anything about the wards at the week-ends.

Do you think hospital staff might be interested in teachers organizing week-end activities for the children?

All seven said that they did not know if the nurses would be interested in the idea, but one mentioned that her children had asked her to come and give them school at the week-ends.

What do you think of staggering school holidays so that the school is never closed?

One thought this was a good idea, especially for the long-stay children who never went home and got thoroughly bored when there was no school. One said that she had experienced this system in another hospital and found it unsatisfactory as there always seemed to be a shortage of staff; the other five disliked such an idea, saying that a 'proper break was needed'.

Do you have regular ward staff/teaching staff meetings on your ward?

Three said that some meetings were held. Four said they never had meetings at all. Regarding meetings for teachers/parents/nurses, all seven said no such meetings were ever held.

Do you know any of the parents of your children?

All seven said they sometimes met the parents when they visited.

Would you be willing to have one or two (not more) seriously subnormal children in your group of physically disabled children?

One teacher said yes. The other six said definitely not, their reasons were: 'my children are of good average intelligence'; 'would impede the teaching of normal children'; 'would seriously impede the constructive work with the other children'; 'unfair to everybody'; two of the six who were against the idea said they had too many reasons against the proposal to even be able to list them, they just knew it would be impossible.

Do you think hospital schools should send school reports home?

One teacher said no, but the other six thought it would be an acceptable idea for long-stay children.

*

People Who Work in Hospitals

Considering the answers given by the teachers the main points to emerge were:

1. *Their lack of interest in child care:* they were just not interested in what happened after school, they did not see it as being any concern of theirs, they did not know what went on and did not go to find out; and they were not interested in organizing out-of-school activities.

2. *Their lack of special qualifications* to do the job, and for which they were being paid an extra increment on their salaries (teaching in Special Schools, which includes hospital schools, carries an extra increment of £137 per year). Courses are available at Colleges of Education and at Universities, but only one of those fourteen teachers had gone on a year's course related to handicapped children.

3. *Their rigid minds with regard to changes in traditional school organization:* they were strongly against accepting seriously subnormal children into their groups, even though when questioned it had been pointed out that the proposal might be part of a scheme to try and disperse seriously subnormal children into other groups in order to see how they could be helped; they were against any changes in the conventional school holiday system. But they were quite happy about bringing in traditional school systems, such as writing school reports, even when up until then that particular hospital had not done so.

4. *Their selfishness:* they showed selfish attitudes most of all in their unwillingness to have their personal free time or holidays interfered with, their emphatic decisions against helping the more seriously mentally handicapped children, and their complete indifference to matters relating to child care in the hospital. To criticize any group of people on an ethical issue such as selfishness is complicated, but the attitudes revealed by the answers of these fourteen teachers are worth drawing attention to because it is a little surprising to find such indifference amongst a group of professional people whose working life is spent amongst handicapped and deprived children. They represented half the staff of a very large hospital school; if this is the attitude of half the teaching staff of all hospitals then will any changes in hospital

child care ever be effected through the informed interest of teachers?

*

These are the comments of some hospital teachers regarding their work with the children and their position in the hospitals.

'If I tread carefully I can make things better'

Miss Y. was the Head of Grange Hospital School, a small suburban hospital accommodating about forty children aged under eleven; most of the children had spina bifida, but sometimes a child with an orthopaedic disorder or cerebral palsy was admitted. The hospital had originally been built as a fever hospital, then it became a long-stay heart hospital, but over recent years it had developed into a hospital home for long-stay children with chronic physical handicaps and social problems; the social problems were usually related to housing, family difficulties or shortage of Special School places. The majority of the children went to the hospital before they were five and stayed until they reached eleven, when they were transferred to another hospital if they still had not got a Special School to go to; the children mostly had average ability mentally. There was always a hard core of about twenty children in the hospital who would probably never be lucky enough to get a place in a Special School, having been turned down by Special School heads because they needed too much physical care for their handicaps or because there were potential behaviour problems.

Miss Y. had only been appointed as Head of the hospital school twelve months before; she said that her first reaction on being shown the hospital had been one of horrified shock that children ever lived in such poor conditions.

There were two long wards, one having the youngest children in it (fives and under); the other having the over-fives. Between the two wards was a square 'day-room'. The wards were bare in the extreme, with iron hospital beds and cots, shabby lockers, hospital counterpanes, glass doors to the outside, and no pictures on the walls, nor curtains anywhere. The sister's office was in a glassed-off section of the youngest children's ward. The centre room, where the children would be during the periods of the day when they were not in school, was also bare, having stacked-up tubular steel chairs in it and their dining tables piled one on top of the other when not in use. There were absolutely no touches of homely comfort, such as pictures, armchairs, cushions, wallpaper or carpets, in this 'day-room'. The toilet and bathroom and linen-cupboards were adjoining this room.

Miss Y. said that the general lack of enthusiasm and the poor physical environment of the place had permeated the classrooms, too, and she had found that the teaching was old-fashioned and colourless. Parent-teacher contact had been nil; because many of the parents rarely visited and were quite unaware of what went on in the hospital, they had just grown used to the idea that their children were handicapped and lived in hospital, and they accepted it; they did not know about the school and nobody had explained it to them.

Miss Y. had just completed a year's course at University and had a Diploma in the Education of Handicapped Children; she also had wide experience in other Special Day Schools. She felt that the first need was to brighten up the schoolrooms, then to make contact with parents, and later on to tactfully try and improve the conditions on the wards.

At the end of her first year Miss Y. held a School open evening. She wrote to all the parents, inviting them to come to the school; she put up a bright display of the children's school work and she prepared coffee and a little buffet supper. The school staff and the Medical Social Worker were there to meet the parents and talk to them, and the organizer of a local Voluntary Society for handicapped children gave a short talk about his Society's work, and stressed how they were always available to help families of handicapped children.

Not all the parents attended the evening, but there was a better response than Miss Y. had anticipated. During the evening she played a tape of the children's school music and the parents listened to this very appreciatively. Two of the children, in wheelchairs, helped to serve round the refreshments; the rest of the children were in the wards, as it was past their bedtime. At the end of the evening Miss Y. gave a talk, introduced a new teacher who was to start in the new term, and thanked the parents for coming; she said that she hoped to arrange another open day to take place in an afternoon, when the children themselves would be able to take part, but this would need a little more planning in order to fit in with the hospital routines.

The parents walked round the classrooms, talked to the teachers and the Medical Social Worker and each other. There was surprise at the standard of the displayed schoolwork, and the fact that the schoolrooms looked just like ordinary school. One parent said, 'This is marvellous, we'd no idea; why, this classroom is better than my youngest boy's infant school, there are some lovely bits of work here.' They felt that it was like a 'proper school' and that their children were getting a chance in spite of being handicapped and living in hospital.

Talking with Miss Y. afterwards she spoke about the difficulties of teaching in such a hospital, and the poor standards of child care. She said that she would like to be able to change the conditions on the wards, but at the moment she was very new and any high-handed critical action by a newcomer would naturally offend the nursing staff and ultimately work against her aims. She had very good relationships with the nursing staff and felt that nothing would be gained by stringent criticisms of nurses who obviously liked the children and tried to do what they thought best for them. But the nurses lacked understanding of what was meant by child care, and their duty hours prevented any lasting individual interest in the children.

Miss Y. thought that more could be done by example than by censure. 'If I tread carefully I can make things better,' she said. She remembered how when she started to brighten up the classrooms and the corridors leading from them, the nurses were pleased at the effect, and said how nice it would be to brighten up the wards as well. Miss Y. hoped that a gradual improvement in the hospital might come from the school department, by concentrating on physically brightening the environment, making good family contact, and maintaining good relationships with the hospital staff.

Miss Y. said that she did not leave school equipment out for using in the wards after school, as it would just become spoiled, and, because the school was equipped and financed by the LEA, she had some responsibility towards them as well as wanting to keep her school stock in usable condition. Lost pieces of puzzle and torn books were of no use to anyone and would give no pleasure to the children. Miss Y. said that she thought there was a great need for some organized occupations, mothering and attention, to be given to the children in the evenings and at week-ends.

'Are hospital teachers merely child-minders?'

Mrs B. was the Head of Villa Hospital, a country hospital which accommodated approximately 100 children who tended to require frequent re-admissions for orthopaedic surgery and medical treatment, and whose stays varied between two weeks and a term. The children who stayed the longest were those who had some social problem which delayed their discharge. Most of the children had good average mental ability. The school-teaching took place in the wards, or in 'day-rooms'; there was one classroom a short distance away from the main ward-blocks. The school worked a four-term year, but did not have staggered holidays; none of the teachers did after-school activities, such as clubs or outings. Two of the teaching staff of ten had special qualifications for teaching handicapped children.

Mrs B. said that she would accept all children, and would never refuse to take a severely subnormal child into a group of ordinary children unless he was completely disruptive and impossible to cope with. 'Nobody could possibly deny a small child, however dull, the *chance* to come and watch the others and dabble his hands in sand and water and listen to music, rather than leave him out of the group, could they?' she asked.

Mrs B. thought the worst problem of hospital teaching was the poor communication between school and hospital staff, and the nurses' lack of understanding about what the teachers were doing with the children. For example, she mentioned student nurses who suddenly cleared up a three-year-old's sand and water play in nursery class and took him out for some treatment which was not necessary at that moment; the nurses did not think it mattered to interrupt his play since in their opinion the child was 'just playing around and not doing anything much'. The nurses often seemed to think that the teachers were there only to keep the children quiet and happy, and did not realize that the children learned as they played and that there was a purpose in the activities that the teachers provided. 'Are hospital teachers merely child-minders?' asked Mrs B., with a frustrated shrug of her shoulders.

A few days later, as I walked around the wards of Villa Hospital, I asked one nurse what Priscilla, a three-year-old in a plaster, did when she was in Nursery School. 'Oh, school? Priscilla? Why nothing. They don't do anything important, just a few toys and things, or playing around with sand,' the nurse replied.

Mrs B. thought that the school holidays and week-ends were bad times for the children as there were so few hospital toys or activities for them, and, in the winter, when the children were shut up for long periods in the wards, the boredom could be intolerable. At least in the summer the two- and three-year-olds in cots had the pleasure of watching the older active children run in and out of the doors on to the courtyard, but in the winter they would not have even this vicarious pleasure, and little would be given to them to play with.

An attempt had once been made at Villa Hospital to solve the problem of occupying the children in the long summer holiday. Student teachers were invited by the hospital to come and spend a month working with the children in the wards. The scheme was organized by the hospital but the school Head went in at the beginning of the students' stay in order to introduce them to the children and loan some equipment. However, after a while, the hospital requested that the entire organization of the student scheme should be taken over by the school; this meant organizing the students' accommodation, writing to the colleges and arranging transport. The school refused to take on this work and eventually the scheme petered out altogether. As neither party could agree about whose responsibility it was to organize occupations in the holidays, a potentially good scheme was permitted to disintegrate, leaving the children still with nothing to do in the holidays.

Discussing the play needs of the children, Mrs B. and her staff, and the Medical Social Worker, all agreed that nurses should receive some definite practical instruction about *how* children play. Some nurses thought they could 'stimulate' a child, and then with every good intent they started to dominate his play, and would not leave him alone, which resulted in his getting tired of trying to think things out for himself. Other nurses piled all the soft toys they could find into the play-pen of a small child and then grumbled at him for throwing them out again. Most of the things the nurses did were meant to be kindly, but they were misguided; and the senior nurses, not themselves understanding the true value of play, did not recognize the mistakes the young nurses were making, or did not think it was very important anyway.

There was good liaison between Mrs B. and the Medical Social Worker, regarding discussions about placing the children in schools and home problems; she said that she knew about individual home problems (in strong contrast to the Head teacher of one very large hospital school, who told me that she did not even know if a certain child had a mother or not, or if she had ever spent a holiday at home).

Mrs B. expressed worry about children who had to undergo frequent periods of in-patient treatment. She thought these children ran a risk of 'exchanging one set of four walls for another' in that they went to hospital and got their treatment (operations, plasters, and so on) and were then discharged home for a few months, but during those few months at home they might have a Home Teacher, in which case they were spending their whole lives in the confines of the four walls of a hospital ward or the four walls of their home. They might not be taken out very much when at home, because of difficulties in carrying them about when in big plasters, or because of the housing, such as upstairs flats or difficult steps impossible to negotiate with a wheel-chair. So these handicapped children, although at home with their parents, were almost as socially isolated as when in hospital.

Would it not be possible for the LEAs to give more aid to

the families of children like this, perhaps in the form of ramps at the door (as recommended in the Bill passed by Parliament in 1970 for aiding the physically handicapped), the loan of a larger car for taking a child in a big plaster, a Voluntary Service 'pusher' to help mother cope with shopping and a wheel-chair? A handicapped child too often has to stay indoors simply because of the sheer physical difficulties of getting him out.

Mrs B. said there was a limit to how much children could learn from books, films, television and radio, and she thought that going out and about should be the concern of hospitals far more than it is at present. One of her teaching staff mentioned how a child of four, who had been in hospital since the age of nearly two (during the period when Villa Hospital took very long-stay children), just did not know what went on inside a normal home; when he arrived home for the first time and saw his mother lighting the fire in the grate he became very apprehensive and asked her anxiously why she lit a bonfire in a room. His only previous experience of fire had been from watching hospital gardeners from the windows of wards when they had bonfires in the grounds.

Mrs. B. did not seem very clear about the role of the teacher in hospital; she emphatically stressed that they were not 'child-minders', and she realized that they played an important part in the lives of the children in hospital, but she saw many insoluble problems connected with staff relationships, staff communication, and the co-ordination of the teachers' work and the hospital staff's work for the benefit of the children.

It seems that the role of the teacher was so ill-determined in Villa Hospital that schemes in which teachers could usefully contribute, or take the lead, were just never going to materialize, despite the teachers talking so coherently about what should be done, e.g. outings, holiday occupations, nurses' instruction in play needs, and so on. Was Villa Hospital not making full use of the potential of its teachers, or were the teachers themselves not offering a positive enough contribution to the hospital? The failure of the students' holiday occupation scheme was a fair example of the two staffs' inability to co-ordinate their aims for the children.

Assistants

The following is a description of a school for seriously subnormal children in a psychiatric hospital, and the comments of its assistant regarding her role in the hospital. The children and the staff and the school in the hospital differ from those in Grange Hospital and Villa Hospital because:

(a) All the children were seriously subnormal mentally, and deemed as 'unsuitable' for education under the DES.

(b) The majority of the children lived permanently in the hospital, having been admitted primarily for long-term care.

(c) The assistant was employed by the Ministry of Health and not the DES.

'How can we teach children who live apart from the world?'

Mrs K.D. was an assistant in the school (Training Centre) of Court Hospital for seriously subnormal children. The school had ten unqualified assistants and a qualified supervisor in charge. Some of the assistants had previous experience with children, e.g. as part-time unqualified nurses or in voluntary work, and some had other work experience, e.g. in office or shop work. There were usually between ten and fourteen children in a class, and each assistant had a class-helper who was a subnormal woman; these subnormal women were brought into the children's hospital daily by coach from an adult hospital and they worked in the wards, the school or the laundries. The school building was purpose-built and new, with light airy rooms, fair cupboard space, peg-board on the walls, a sink in each room, little chairs and tables for the younger children, plus tables for the teachers.

Mrs K.D. was middle-aged, with two adolescent children of her own, and she lived locally. She had first become familiar with the hospital through voluntary work and helping with the subnormal children in the wards; then, having got interested in the children, she applied for a job in the school.

Her hours were from 9.30 to approximately 11.30 and in the afternoons from 1.30 until 4 o'clock. She received about £15 per week, and had six weeks' holiday a year. She said the work was tiring but not hard, and she was satisfied with the salary, the hours and holidays. The holidays were staggered so that the school closed completely for only one week in the year, in order that the children did not have long periods without school. This arrangement meant a certain amount of give-and-take between the assistants, and sometimes a little sharing of children, but with voluntary help and students in the summer they managed to organize it quite well.

Mrs K.D. had been at Court Hospital for two years and had just been accepted for a training course to obtain the Diploma of the National Association of Mental Health in teaching mentally handicapped children. In her class she had fourteen children aged from eight to ten, and a nineteen-year-old girl with mongolism as her permanent class-helper.

Around the walls of the classroom there were finger paintings, pictures made of materials such as cut-up egg boxes, and some drawn and coloured pictures which Mrs K.D. had prepared herself and written words beneath. In one corner there was a sink, in another a sand-tray, and in a third a battered Wendy House containing some dressing-up clothes, and two little chairs and a tiny table. As we talked the children sat around us on the floor looking at old wallpaper books, or playing with inset puzzle toys or throwing sand about the room. Now and again a small boy came and pulled at my handbag, repeating, 'Money, money' and nodding his head. 'That's all he says,' Mrs K.D. remarked.

At mid-morning the class-helper sat all the children round a table and gave them each a small bottle of milk and a straw; she did this very slowly and carefully and was censorious with any small child who fidgeted about at the table. While they drank their milk she fetched a bag of chocolate buttons and counted out three for each child.

Mrs K.D. said that she was looking forward to doing her Diploma course; she had had a few opportunities to attend an occasional lecture, but not as many chances as she would have liked, so the full-time course would be a marvellous opportunity. She wondered exactly what the course would equip her for, however; whether it would really help her to work with hospitalized children, or whether it would be biased towards children who lived in their own homes and had an ordinary life.

Occasionally Mrs K.D. stopped talking, to wipe a child's nose or to stop a child running out of the room. She said that she very seldom saw the parents of the children; some of the children never had visits from their parents at all as they were completely rejected by their families, or else the families lived too far away to visit very often.

Mrs K.D. explained that the children did not have any idea of *how to play*, and she spoke of a little girl who came in daily from home and had far more idea of things in general and was more advanced in her speech and play, although her psychological test actually showed her as having a lower I.Q. than the other children in the class. This particular little girl then ran over to us; she was a friendly, neat little seven-year-old with mongolism, and she held Mrs K.D.'s arm and chatted repetitively.

'You do see such a difference in the children who come daily from home; we've got about four who live at home and they can do so much more than the others,' Mrs K.D. said. She then showed me the Wendy House and said the children just did not know what to do in it. I asked if this might be because the children never saw 'home things' in the wards.

'Of course,' she replied, 'they never see *anything* homelike going on in the wards, so how can they know what to play at in the Wendy House?'

She was particularly dissatisfied with the pictures she had been given as part of her school stock; they all represented home situations, such as sweeping, cooking, washing in individual bedroom hand-basins, posting letters, a mother doing ironing and so on. 'These pictures mean *nothing* to these ward children, absolutely nothing at all; they never experience these sorts of things,' Mrs K.D. said bitterly. 'How can we teach children who live apart from the world?'

Looking at a picture of children posting letters into a bright red letter box, I asked: 'How about that, have you ever taken the children down to the letter box at the end of the hospital drive? Then they would connect the picture with the outing and it would be something you would be able to talk about to them.'

She said, regretfully, that in her two years' teaching at the school she had never taken any of the children out to the shops or to post a letter. She wondered about the reaction of other people: 'Do outsiders accept children like this?' 'Don't you think more publicity is needed so that people won't stare?' She said that personally she would be most willing to take one or two children to the supermarket when she did her weekly shopping, but she would need staff to help her. Mrs K.D.'s difficulties were obvious, for, shut in a classroom with fourteen seriously subnormal children, it was a puzzle to know what else she could do other than attempt to copy traditional infant-school techniques, such as sitting the children at tables to do some painting, a bit of scribbling and so on. No matter how interested she might be, her role under those circumstances could be little more than custodian-cum-pseudo teacher.

At lunch-time we walked back to the wards with the children. One ward had been structurally adapted for a research experiment a few years previously, when a group of children had been given an improved environment and more individual mothering, bunk beds, pictures on the walls, better eating arrangements and so on. But the children from Mrs K.D.'s class came from an original ward. This ward had an elderly sister, who met us at the door with the greeting: 'Oh, my goodness, a visitor, and we are all in a frightful muddle this morning and such a mess.'

Sister had a dark dress, starched apron, shiny belt and starched cap. She was flustered at our arrival and ushered the children hastily into the 'potty room'; this room had the inevitable rows of yellow plastic pots on the floor, upon which all the children were immediately placed. All the rooms were immaculate; the dining-room was spotless, bare of pictures and ornaments and toys, with only the formica-topped tables and the chairs in it. The bedroom had twenty beds in it, arranged with reverent symmetry, each having a small locker beside it; pleasant curtains, well-kept paint, and bright counterpanes made a clean wholesome scene, but there were no toys or clothes visible, no pictures or books, not a shoe or slipper in sight; it was difficult to believe that this room was the bedroom and permanent home of twenty backward children. It was more like a store room for hospital beds, being kept clean and ready for some expected national disaster. It was clear that no germs were harboured; it was not a home. What was so incredible was that this ward was barely a stone's-throw away from the research ward, whose findings continued to uphold the theories that an institutional environment is detrimental to human development.

Why was more value *still* put on the old hospital routines rather than on homeliness, *despite* all the findings of researchers? Do sisters fear the unruliness of children when allowed to 'make a mess', have toys around, and be normally untidy? One young nurse who had worked on the research ward said: 'It was awful when that research thing was being run, the children got so much attention and were allowed to do as they liked and make a mess; they started showing-off and got ever so noisy and spoilt, really naughty they were.'

Nurses

Today's nurses are not always unmarried career women. The shortage of staff, particularly in long-stay hospitals for the chronically handicapped, and the trend for married women to work mean that today there are many married middle-aged part-time unqualified 'nurses' working in long-stay hospitals. Their work does not involve nursing surgical or acute patients; they are generally employed in wards accommodating children with chronic physical and/or mental handicaps. They wear a uniform, are often called 'nurse' by the staff and children, and are known as nursing auxiliaries in some hospitals and as nursing aides in others. Their work covers the general day-to-day care of the children – bathing, washing, toileting, helping with meals and feeding, seeing to clothes, making beds, sorting bed-linen, cleaning pots and trolleys. The work is often heavy and tiring, specially if physically handicapped adolescents are involved; the continual lifting of fully grown helpless adolescent boys and girls from baths, beds and wheel-chairs can cause back-ache and be exhausting; the care of the seriously subnormal can also be a mental and physical strain.

Nursing auxiliaries do not take full responsibility for the ward they work on, although they may be employed there for many years and know exactly what needs doing. The person in overall charge is usually a State Registered Nurse, or a State Enrolled Nurse. They will be responsible for writing reports, seeing to special diets, giving out drugs, controlling nursing and domestic staff and visitors, and general administration of the ward.

In addition to the married unqualified staff and the qualified senior nurses, a large proportion of the staff on long-stay wards may be young women filling in time before beginning their proper nursing training, or students who are waiting to go to College to begin training as teachers, physiotherapists, doctors, etc.; these 'nurses' will only be temporary; in most long-stay hospitals there is a continuous flow of unqualified students, both English and overseas, who may work in the wards for any time varying from six weeks to a year. There are also a number of young overseas visitors, especially from Scandinavia, who get jobs as temporary unqualified nurses for about six months, solely in order to learn English.

The unmarried qualified 'career nurses' – the sisters, staff nurses and the State Enrolled Nurses – sometimes go on to study an aspect of nursing which specially qualifies them to work in a long-stay hospital, e.g. they may get a qualification in psychiatric nursing. But nursing short-stay acutely ill patients is generally the more popular side of nursing, as opposed to the day-to-day care of the incurably disabled or subnormal. Nursing in one of the big famous Teaching Hospitals, or a modern cancer hospital or heart hospital can be much more exciting from a medical point of view than the care of chronically handicapped children in one of the old Poor Law Institutions or fever hospitals.

So, there tend to be two streams of nurses: first, the 'career nurses' with the better qualifications who will seek appointments in the more interesting hospitals: secondly, the part-timers, the unqualified, the married women who want a few hours' work a week, the students and the language learners, who will work in the long-stay hospitals.

The following pages give brief descriptions, comments and opinions of some nurses who work with handicapped children.

*'They're well-fed – the food is lovely,
what else can you do for them?'*

Nurse Jones was a part-time nurse in her forties, with two adolescent boys of her own. She had become a nurse in order to earn a little extra money for the family, and had been working as a nursing auxiliary for four years in a ward for fifteen long-stay physically handicapped children. The children were all handicapped through cerebral palsy; some were totally handicapped, half needed help with feeding and toileting, there were a lot of speech disabilities and some deafness, and several children had behaviour problems. Their mental abilities varied from very low (subnormal) to above average.

Nurse Jones said that she had passed a few Red Cross exams but knew nothing about hospitals and handicapped children when she had applied for the job; what she now knew she had 'just picked up' since she had been working in the ward. During her first week in the hospital she had been taken on a tour of the different departments, laundries, linen rooms, and so on, in order to know what went on in a hospital. On her first day the ward sister had told her about the children's handicaps. She had never been asked to attend any lectures on handicapped children or the needs of children who were away from their families, and she had never received any instruction in child care or about how to occupy children. But she remembered going one afternoon to see a film in the hospital hall: 'It was a physiotherapy film and showed you how to carry and feed a spastic child.' She said that when she had first started working there she had not known what to expect and thought she would never get used to the work because the heavily handicapped children had horrified and depressed her, but now the work never worried her at all and she liked the children.

Asked if she thought a hospital was really a suitable place for children to live when they were not ill, but only physically handicapped, Nurse Jones said that she really had not thought about it. It was difficult to say, she supposed that they had to be *somewhere*, it was just a good job that there were hospitals to take the children. If she had had a handicapped child herself she could not say how she would have reacted, so she could not blame parents for leaving children in hospital.

Asked what improvements she would like to see made, she said most of all it would be to be called 'Aunty' or 'Mrs Jones', rather than 'nurse'. She would also like to have uniforms abolished, and the 'ridiculous hats'. But if uniforms were abolished she would want a dress allowance. She did not think there were many improvements that could be made in the wards for the children; she thought they were well fed and clean.

Asked if she was satisfied about the feeding arrangements Nurse Jones said again that the food was very good. But when asked specifically if she was satisfied with the actual meal *arrangements* – the bare tables, the adults standing there watching the children eat, and the fact that children never saw food cooked or adults sitting down and eating – Nurse Jones asked, 'Do children notice?' I pointed out that if children lived permanently like that then they were being deprived of a normal family-style of life, and Nurse Jones replied that this had never occurred to her, she supposed on thinking about it that it might be better to do things differently, but what else could they do?

'After all,' she said, 'we're always short-staffed, the main thing is to get the food down the difficult feeders and have done with it, we're always in too much of a hurry to fuss about things.' (It was difficult to understand Nurse Jones's hurry as there was an empty waiting period of well over an hour between the children finishing lunch and going back into school.)

Asked if she had ever visited a Residential Special School for handicapped children and seen the system of houseparents and the more leisurely way that the children lived, eating at individual family-group tables with their houseparents, Nurse Jones said that she had never visited any other places or schools and had no idea about houseparents, but she thought 'it sounds like a quite good idea, if only you have the time'.

Nurse Jones saw her work in the hospital as mainly a type of domestic work, i.e. cleaning pots, tidying beds, and so on. Asked if she had any duties specially concerned with looking after the children's toys, Nurse Jones said that nobody had to do anything about the toys, but sometimes they sorted out bits of puzzles;

they never had to mend books or sharpen pencils. As regards personal responsibilities connected with the children Nurse Jones said she sometimes had to mend clothes, but she never did any personal washing for the children, and did not take any responsibility for outings or occupations. Any duties she had were merely set ward duties connected with *things*, rather than with the children. She said that her work suited her, as she liked the money coming in, and she would hate to have real responsibility. It did not bother her that each day proceeded in the same way, with a round of set duties, and no follow-up of individual interests with the children, such as plans of things to do that would carry over into the next day.

The children obviously liked and trusted Nurse Jones. She was essentially a very kindly woman; she said she had become very fond of the children and often thought about them when she was not working, and she felt sad about their handicaps. It did not occur to her to look critically at the hospital care of long-stay children, and she thought of child care solely in terms of food and shelter. 'After all,' she emphasized, 'they're well-fed – the food is lovely, what else can you do for them? The food is beautifully served, not all mixed up in a muddle on their plates.'

'It just gets a habit to say there is no time'

Sister Smith was in her thirties, and in charge of a very busy ward accommodating more than twenty children who were in hospital for orthopaedic surgery. The children were all suffering from permanent physical handicaps – spine, limb, hip disabilities – but they were not long-stay in-patients and their stay in Sister Smith's ward was only between two weeks and four months. They would have frequent re-admissions, so most of them were well-known to the sister.

Sister Smith said that nursing in a surgical ward was far more interesting work than working with long-term seriously subnormal children in one of the big old Institutions. Work in a psychiatric hospital would not appeal to her at all because it just meant the day-to-day looking after of physically well children and it was not real nursing; she had qualified to be a nurse and would always choose surgical work.

She said that her nurses did not occupy the children as much as they ought to do on Saturday and Sunday mornings because treatments had to be done, such as dressings, but the afternoons were a bit more interesting for the children as they were wheeled outside in the hospital grounds.

Asked if she missed the teachers during the holidays Sister Smith said definitely not as she found the children were far easier to manage when they did not have school all day. She thought school made the children fractious and wild in the week-day evenings, and she blamed this on the school being 'repressive', which meant that as soon as it was finished the children felt released and then started to 'let off steam'. But because children in hospital cannot rush about the roads and playgrounds and their gardens as they would do at home (most of Sister Smith's children were in plasters and traction) all their pent-up energy had to be used up in quarrels and over-excitement.

Sister Smith said that she thought the saying that there was 'never any time' was used thoughtlessly by too many nurses. 'It just gets a habit to say there is no time,' she remarked. 'After all, how long does it take to read a child a story? Five minutes? No nurse is too busy to spare five minutes now and again.' She thought nurses should take care that the excuse about 'no time' was not being just a cover-up for their lack of interest in the children.

She saw her role with handicapped children as being essentially one of nursing, and wanted to make the fullest use of her professional skill as a nurse; at the same time, she thought that no child should be swamped under hospital routines and she was not averse to criticizing the system if it threatened to do so.

'These kids get more than I ever did'

Sister Bertram was elderly, and had trained to work with seriously subnormal children. She was in charge of a ward for long-stay physically handicapped children, some of whom had mental handicaps as well although several of the children were above average in intelligence. The children were aged from two to sixteen; some of them lived permanently in the ward and had social problems related to family, housing and difficulties in school placement. The hospital was very large and was in a country district; it had been built in the 1880s as a fever hospital.

Sister Bertram lived in the hospital, she had few friends and no family of her own as she had been orphaned at an early age and brought up in a large old-style orphanage. She thought that children in hospital had a marvellous time and never tired of comparing their lives to her own meagre childhood in the orphanage.

'Look at all the sweets and toys these children get, look at the nice party they have at Christmas, and their outing to the sea in the summer. *I* never got anything like that when I was a child.' The children in Sister Bertram's ward usually had four collective outings by coach in every year.

Sister Bertram showed no originality in the way that she arranged her ward; in comparison to some other wards in the same hospital it was bare and ugly. She had no family home experiences of her own upon which she could draw as a pattern for organizing her ward; and, because as a child she had never experienced the affection of one adult, she never saw any need for the hospital children to have any one adult caring for them, such as a housemother, in spite of the fact that they often spent their whole childhood on her ward.

She had an authoritarian attitude to the children and her staff, and little patience with children who whined or who had come from homes where mother had 'spoilt' them: 'You mustn't give in to children, ever,' she would say, 'it's really wicked to spoil children.'

When a child was once crying with a throat infection she told her that when *she* had been a little girl there had never been nice antibiotic tablets, only a hot water bottle for her swollen neck. Her own deprived experiences in a children's orphanage had coloured all her attitude to the children in her care: 'These kids get more than I ever did, they don't know how lucky they are,' she would say.

Occasionally she would suddenly go out and spend a considerable part of her not very large salary on buying clothes for one of the more deprived children. On these occasions she evoked feelings of pity from her staff. At other times her staff alternated between nervousness or amusement at her inconsistencies. In consideration of the fact that psychological researches have postulated that early deprivation can result in a child developing a neurotic personality, and may have irreversible effects on a person's ability to form warm and lasting relationships, it is a poor reflection on the administration of the hospital that such a deprived woman as Sister Bertram should have been placed in charge of a group of long-stay deprived children. Her role in her ward was negative; she found it difficult to do anything other than reproduce deprived conditions similar to those she had experienced as a child, and to take great pains never to 'spoil' (i.e. give affection to) a child. Her own deprivations were being constantly re-lived and perpetuated on to yet another generation. It would have seemed more expedient to have placed Sister Bertram on an out-patient department, or in a very short-stay ward where she would not have to take responsibility for home-making and child care.

'Teachers carry germs'

Sister Cook was near retirement and in charge of an orthopaedic ward which accommodated boys for both long- and short-stay surgical treatment. She was notorious for her rigid views about visiting, but had had to concede to the relaxed visiting regulations regarding parents. Realizing that she had lost her battle as regards *parents* in the ward, she strengthened her hand against *other* types of visitors, i.e. non-related ones. On one occasion a hospital teacher from another department attempted to visit a boy aged five who had been transferred to Sister Cook's ward for an operation. The teacher was met at the ward door by the stout, fierce figure of Sister Cook and promptly refused entry. When asked why, for the child was expecting her, the teacher was told: 'I don't allow teachers to visit. Teachers carry germs. Only parents are allowed in.'

The teacher protested that the child did not have a family, he had been in her department for several years and knew her best of all, and she was sure he would want to see somebody he knew.

But Sister Cook only reiterated her maxim that 'teachers carry germs'.

That small boy spent nearly a month on Sister Cook's ward before returning to his own department, but in that time he did not have a visitor, because Sister Cook maintained her ban on teachers and he had nobody else. Because *set* visiting hours had been abandoned to allow free access for parents there was no official hour in which the teachers could have *insisted* on visiting so Sister Cook was in complete control of the situation. Such a situation could have been thought of as ludicrous, for Sister Cook was akin to a music-hall caricature of a traditional hospital sister, but the fact that her rigid rules affected a child quickly detracted from any amusement one might have felt at her odd behaviour. She was apparently an excellent, well-qualified and clever sister as regards the nursing of surgical cases; she apparently also saw her role as being a defender of the old hospital traditions.

'Who defends a homeless child against radical medical decisions?'

Charge Nurse Johns was a male nurse aged fifty. He had worked for more than ten years in charge of a long-stay ward for boys handicapped by muscular dystrophy, aged fifteen to twenty. He had made many improvements in their ward during those years, despite the old-fashioned hospital structure. He had made the boys' 'day-room' into a comfortable dining-room/lounge; there were travel and pin-up pictures on the walls, and shelves round the room for hobbies, radios, books and magazines. There was a lot of freedom at mealtimes, the boys had their supper when they wanted it, and breakfast was cooked individually as the boys got up and decided what they wanted. It had not been easy to make improvements, as other wards in the hospital retained their traditional customs and Charge Nurse Johns had faced considerable lack of sympathy for his ideas. He was lucky in that he had a nucleus of permanent staff working with him, and there was also very good cooperation between the teachers and the nurses on the ward.

He said that, thinking of the problems facing long-stay deprived children, he felt particular concern for the way in which very important medical decisions could be taken which often shaped a child's whole future but in which the child would have no say. A child with parents would have them question a surgeon about the necessity of an operation, but a child without a family risked undergoing all sorts of treatments which he might look back on as an adult and wish had not taken place, for instance an amputation. 'Who defends a homeless child against radical medical decisions?'

Charge Nurse Johns thought that many problems facing long-stay children could be averted if there were more social workers maintaining family contact; he blamed many of the troubles on a shortage of social workers in hospitals and Local Authorities. He knew social workers himself who had so many clients on their books that they rarely managed thoroughly to know their problems. He thought the main answer to the shortage of staff was to give all people who worked with handicapped people – social workers, houseparents, nurses and teachers – a much higher salary.

He said that he would prefer to be a housefather in a Residential Home or Special School, or would like to be in charge of a Hostel for handicapped boys; then he could really put into practice all the home and community ideas that chronically handicapped young people should have. But he just could not afford to live on the low salary he would be paid as a housefather (a senior houseparent in a Local Authority Hostel or Home receives a salary of between £700 and £880 per year). So, for the moment, he would stay in the hospital and carry on what he was doing in his self-appointed role of housefather-cum-hospital nurse, trying to make the ward as much like home as possible for the boys.

An Occupation–Play Therapist

Mrs Webb was in her late forties and had adolescent children of her own. She had been working in the hospital for more than ten years. The hospital was mainly for children needing medical treatment, for tuberculosis, asthma, cystic fibrosis, heart disease, and so on; these children tended to keep coming back into hospital for periods of six weeks to three months. There were also a few children who were admitted for orthopaedic surgery.

Mrs Webb had at one time been a handicraft teacher, with a private school of her own. She had been appointed to her hospital job to provide handiwork occupations for the children in after-school hours and during school holidays. During her first two years there she had worked at the week-ends because at that time there were a number of very active children who had got so thoroughly bored that they were getting into mischief which was bordering on being dangerous. Now she only worked in the week. Her hours were from 9.15 until about 5, and she had four weeks' holiday a year. She worked with approximately thirty children, splitting them into small groups or working individually with them. There were four teachers in the hospital, and one other 'occupation–play therapist'.

Mrs Webb found that much of her work overlapped with the work of the teachers, and she worked in collaboration with them. She gave the children occupations such as basket-work, leather-work, lampshade making, clay modelling, toys, puzzles, painting, collage making, drawing, ball games in the grounds, walks through the woods and trips to the local shops. She gave considerable aid to the physiotherapists regarding the medical needs of the children, such as chest exercises, movement in the open air and assistance with swimming.

She found that her role in relation to the nursing staff was a little difficult to define because the junior nurses and State Enrolled Nurses sometimes resented having to work 'under' someone who was not a qualified nurse. Mrs Webb thought there was frequently a lack of understanding of children in hospitals, particularly amongst the younger nursing staff; all their training was orientated to the basic rules of hospital nursing, i.e. performance of duties rather than child care. She thought that the nurses in their late teens and early twenties were much further away from understanding childhood than the older women. She found it especially galling when young nurses left the children's toys around the ward quite uncared for and getting spoilt and then just pushed them away all in a muddle in a cupboard. Little matters like caring for toys were important because it meant pleasure and occupation for the children; there was nothing worse than a cupboard full of broken toys.

Mrs Webb said that one difficulty of hospital life was how to keep the *reality of home* fresh in the child's mind. She found that the children built up their homes to be absolute Utopias, embellishing their memories with ideas that were quite unrealistic. Even the short-stay children were inclined to do this. (I have found this to be a common characteristic for long-stay children.) On arrival home the children were often bitterly disappointed at what they found; neither the material standards nor the family relationships came up to their expectations. She thought the 'spoiling' of children in hospital – all the professional attention they received from adults looking at them and handling them – made them very demanding and precocious. Then, when they went home and mother was not able to give them that sort of attention, they were disappointed with their home. Mrs Webb said that children who had to spend a lot of time going in and out of hospitals should have help with keeping in touch with the rough-and-tumble of family life, i.e. mother getting bad-tempered, having to live in small cramped houses, father daily rushing off to work and so on. It would be difficult to know how this could be done, but it would be helped if more week-ends at home could be arranged.

Mrs Webb saw her role in the hospital as definitely not being one of mothering the children; she was very wary of giving affection that might usurp the place of mother. She looked on her role as an occupier and a mediator of fair play; when many of the children were only in the hospital for check-ups and observation and were active and running about, there was often a very explosive and quarrelsome atmosphere. Mrs Webb found that one of her main functions was to sort out their quarrels and see that every child got his fair share of attention and was listened to in the arguments that occurred. Giving them interesting occupations was one way of avoiding the inevitable quarrels.

'Everlastingly I am soothing out petty quarrels, this one has taken that one's best toy, so-and-so has said something insulting. So, I smooth out the quarrels and see to fair play for them.'

The value of Mrs Webb's work could be appreciated when one looked round the hospital and imagined it in wet or cold weather. It was right out in the country, surrounded by thick woods. The nurses were busy, there were usually some operations taking place or post-operative care being given. The wards were small and very cramped. Under these conditions there was likely to be constant bickering unless some special adult could be relied upon to try and sort things out. Children's quarrels might seem trivial, but they are important to the children involved in them, and can assume mountainous proportions of stress if not sorted out. Some of the tense quarrelsome situations recorded in the diaries of the ward children would not have occurred had there been a Mrs Webb to soothe matters.

The Role of the Voluntary Worker in Long-stay Children's Hospitals

The deficiencies described in this study have sometimes been caused by the pressures of genuine staff shortages, but sometimes by staff organization, e.g. rules which forbid a nurse to leave her ward to help push children on an outing, even though if the children are taken out there would not *be* any children left on that ward for her to look after.

When staff shortages cannot be eased, or the rules cannot be abolished, then the use of voluntary workers may be a means of improving child care. The value of the voluntary worker in the social services has long been recognized, and Government Reports on the various social services generally pay tribute to the help that volunteers give. In the Report of the Committee on Local Authority and Allied Personal Social Services it is stated: 'Volunteers have an important role to play in residential institutions, such as hospitals . . .' and, 'We are not suggesting that volunteers can replace professional workers but that they can assume, within the framework of the service and with some preparation, many of the duties that need not be carried out by a qualified professional worker . . .' and, '. . . we have no doubt of the social value of voluntary work . . . in showing concern . . . and so demonstrating community acceptance. . . .'

The following discussion refers to some aspects of the role of the voluntary worker in long-stay hospitals for children.

The Work of a Co-ordinator of Voluntary Services in a Children's Hospital

Voluntary Services Co-ordinators, or Organizers of Voluntary Services in Hospitals, have been appointed in British hospitals since 1951, but there is no compulsion for a hospital to make such an appointment and less than 100 hospitals have done so (1970). The appointment can be filled by a man or woman; some may have qualifications in social work, others have personnel or management experience; the work comes into the category of administration and the salary is between £1,300 and £1,700 per year (1970).

It may be argued whether such an appointment is necessary; is it just another instance of our twentieth-century preoccupation with the need to specialize and create professions? Do such appointments fragment the social services even more, making yet another profession for the consumer to get entangled with? Could the work not be performed adequately by the hospital Medical Social Workers themselves? Such arguments may have a certain validity. However, the first priority of the professional Medical Social Worker always lies with her 'client' – patient, parent, relative – and although appreciating the help given by volunteers she may rarely have the time to organize the voluntary work into any coherent and useful pattern. Consequently, many voluntary workers have been lost, perhaps falling out because they felt unwanted and awkward. A person may have to muster up a lot of courage to volunteer help in a hospital, and it only needs a slight rebuff to make a volunteer shrug his shoulders and disappear. The Voluntary Services Co-ordinator can prevent this because his prime function is making the best use of voluntary workers. He is the link between the hospital and the volunteer, he introduces the volunteer to the different departments, gives information about the work there is to do, introduces the staff to the volunteer and makes sure that all offers of help are used in the wisest way. He 'professionalizes' the volunteers, giving them official acceptance and making them hospital workers in their own right, so that they no longer have to creep apologetically into the hospital wondering whether they are welcome or not.

Mrs MacDonald, the newly appointed Voluntary Services Coordinator of a large hospital for children, stressed that she had three streams of loyalty: first, to the children, then to the hospital staff and then to her volunteers. She felt that she was in a unique position to smooth out misunderstandings which might take place between hospital staff and voluntary workers. While her role was to maintain relationships between the two factions it was not at the same time to cover up hospital deficiencies if they existed; she thought the voluntary workers represented an articulate and highly perceptive section of the community and their opinions should be considered. But she did not see volunteers in any way as a pressure group aimed at influencing hospital policy, she thought that their prime purpose was to give *practical* help to patients. In Mrs MacDonald's hospital they were 'an extra pair of hands', essentially involved with being with the children; they pushed the children out in wheel-chairs, played with them in the wards, helped in the swimming pool with dressing and undressing, helped with feeding and washing helpless children.

Mrs MacDonald said that one important aspect of her work was to try and educate the local public about the hospital, through schools, women's clubs, Church groups, and so on. She sometimes lectured to clubs and schools. She was particularly interested in encouraging young people from local schools to work in the hospital, for they were going to be the the future parents, nurses, teachers, social workers and doctors, and if they had experienced working with handicapped children it would serve to break down prejudice about handicaps. Mrs MacDonald arranged for senior school children to work in the wards after school, and they helped to feed subnormal babies, played with the children and cleaned shoes. They had to be over fifteen to work in the wards; but they were allowed to help the assistants and supervisors in the school for seriously subnormal children when they were fourteen.

Mrs MacDonald said that the value of voluntary work depended on its consistency, and requests by a volunteer to undertake very personal work in the nature of being an 'aunty' to a deprived child had to be very carefully considered. She tried to impress on volunteer 'aunties' that their visits *had* to be consistent, and at the same time they were to realize that they must in no way try to supplant the child's rightful mother.

A fair proportion of Mrs MacDonald's day was spent in interviewing prospective volunteers, showing parties round the hospital, talking to visitors, and contacting representatives of local associations and statutory services. Voluntary Services Co-ordinators work in cooperation with the Local Authority social services, sometimes arranging for voluntary drivers to go on journeys which may not come under the official Hospital Car Service – escorting a child to or from an out-patient clinic, or home at weekends, or fetching parents from the local station or even from their own homes when visiting. One large hospital for children uses approximately fifty voluntary drivers to supplement the regular Hospital Car Service.

All Voluntary Services Co-ordinators work in close contact with associations that will provide voluntary workers, such as youth clubs, Church groups, Scouts and Guides, the National Association for the Welfare of Children in Hospital, Rotary Clubs, Leagues of Friends, the WRVS, and so on. And there are also people who do not belong to associations but who have time to spend a few hours each week in helping in a hospital: perhaps middle-aged housewives whose families have grown up, or retired people. Apparently there is no shortage of voluntary workers.

In some hospitals the voluntary workers wear uniforms, in order to avoid confusion with other staff and so that they can be distinguished from trespassers in a ward. But Mrs MacDonald thought that as long-stay children were surrounded by uniforms all the time it was better if volunteers in children's hospitals wore ordinary clothes; by seeing 'normal' clothes the children's experiences were widened.

Using Voluntary Workers in a Hospital School

Two teachers in a long-stay children's hospital were concerned that the children they taught never went out regularly; sometimes a whole term or more would go by without their leaving the hospital at all. All the school teaching material – books, reading aids

People Who Work in Hospitals 189

and mathematics material – were geared to the day-to-day things that ordinary children experienced as a matter of course as they went to school and back, or out with their friends and parents; but the hospital children never had these experiences. For a hospital child to sit in a room trying to learn to read from a book with gay pictures of posting letters and buying sweets, when he never left the hospital walls, was as irrelevant to his experiences as trying to teach him to read from a book devoted to illustrations about splitting the atom.

It was decided that shopping outings would have to be organized. It was hoped that three children could go on one morning each week; with between twelve and eighteen children in that particular department, it would mean that each child's turn would only come about once in every three to four weeks, but the outings would be more enjoyable if kept to small numbers. Early difficulties arose because the headmistress opposed the scheme on the grounds that school time was a period which had to be used in classroom work and she thought that going shopping was a waste of time, but these disagreements were successfully resolved. The next difficulty arose because of transport. Hospital transport (coach or ambulance) was available only after a lot of pleading and then it was only very grudgingly given, and liable to be cancelled at a few minutes' notice and thus disappoint expectant children. Initially, an administrator of the hospital League of Friends personally transported the children to the town in his own car, with three wheel-chairs bulging out of his car-boot. A year later the hospital agreed to provide regular transport, and three years after that the school bought a mini-bus of its own.

The third difficulty was finding the staff to help to push the children's chairs. Hospital staff were not available because it would mean nurses leaving the ward, despite the fact that there were no children in that department's ward during school time (when the trips would be taken) and the nurses themselves openly admitted to being bored and having nothing to do during school hours. Eventually it was decided to use voluntary helpers. The hospital did not have a Voluntary Services Co-ordinator, so one of the teachers concerned in the scheme contacted the local Parent–Teacher Association and a Church group, and collected some half dozen 'pushers'. The job of pushing needed a strong pair of arms, and the person also had to be a 'jack-of-all-trades' for there were noses to wipe, incoherent requests to decipher from children with speech defects, steps to negotiate in the hilly town, and small children to comfort when they got scared of large dogs and noisy buses. Taking very handicapped children into public toilets and feeding helpless dribbling children in public restaurants also posed some problems.

Most of the helpers were middle-aged women, but several were young and had children of their own at primary school. One had trained as a nurse before her marriage, another worked in a hospital laboratory, the others had no experience of handicapped children before volunteering; in spite of the fact that the children were grossly handicapped, some being mentally as well as physically disabled, none of the helpers cancelled her offer to help; they have continued to support the scheme for more than four years. A rota of times is always kept, and any helper who has a particular interest in any child is always allowed to push him. Many of the children have made friends with their 'pushers' and have gone to their homes with them.

The local town, after having got over its initial interest, soon accepted the regular outing from the hospital, and nobody stared any longer. Instead, there was a lot of practical help and friendliness. The children went to one large restaurant as regular customers and were made welcome by the waitresses, although they were messy eaters and their wheel-chairs took up a lot of room. Sometimes small disasters occurred, as when a shaking spastic hand grabbed at a supermarket display of tinned goods, and a five-year-old had a tantrum because she could not buy a television set, but nearly every trip was a success.

In the beginning, the younger children sometimes cried when they were first taken out, as they had been in hospital for so long that the noise and strangeness of the town badly frightened them (these children were aged four and five). But, as the outings persisted, their confidence increased and these very timid children also began to show an improvement in their language development.

Favourite things to do in the town have been: going into a cake shop and buying doughnuts and looking at long loaves; waiting at the bus-stop for the conductor to ring the bell, and watching passengers go upstairs; smelling soap at cosmetic counters; examining packs of steak, kidney, liver and tripe from the cold storage meat display in supermarkets; having their wheel-chairs pushed into dark and weirdly lit teenage clothes stores; feeling candlewick counterpanes on beds; counting the knives in shop windows; watching traffic lights change; looking at an old man's hearing aid (several of the children had never before believed that adults could have a handicap, being always surrounded by physically healthy young professional staff); going to a launderette with the school dolls' clothes.

Stories about towns at last began to have some real meaning to these children, and they also made lots of outside friends. Some of the children who went on these trips were aged thirteen and over and had spent more than nine years in hospital.

In a hospital which accommodates approximately 1,000 patients, many of them being long-stay, this small group of a dozen children are the only ones who have *regular* weekly outings to the local town. The trips were made possible only because of the help of voluntary workers.

The Work of a Hospital 'Aunty'

Mrs Arnold was in her early sixties, she had a grown-up family and an energetic elderly husband. Five years ago, Mrs Arnold volunteered, through the Townswomen's Guild, to help in the League of Friends' canteen in her local children's hospital, but what she had really wanted to do was 'something, however menial, with the children themselves'. So she saw the Medical Social Worker (there was not a Voluntary Services Co-ordinator) who arranged for her to be an 'aunty' to Joe, a ten-year-old totally handicapped, but intelligent, cerebral palsied child. He had already been in the hospital for three years; he had never stood, he was unable to speak, he could not hold anything in his hands, he could not even hold up his head. He had a wheel-chair and could be taken out if securely strapped in. He needed feeding, washing, undressing, everything had to be done for him; he was also in nappies as he was incontinent.

Joe had not had an 'aunty' before, and his mother's visits were only very brief and irregular. Mrs Arnold saw him first in his ward, and 'took to him straightaway'. Ever since that first meeting she has visited him twice a week, and spends about two to three hours with him. If anything has ever occurred which has meant that she has had to cancel a visit (which is rare in her well-ordered life) then she has always telephoned the ward and arranged another date. She said that the most important thing is to be consistent. Mrs Arnold has not had much personal contact with Joe's mother, but sometimes their visits have coincided and on these occasions Mrs Arnold has slipped away. She thought it was not right to try and replace mother, and in her conversations with Joe she always tried to keep his mother 'alive' for him. She had the impression that Joe's mother was almost afraid of the child's dreadful handicaps and she always seemed in a hurry to get away, never staying for more than fifteen minutes or so. Far from resenting the 'aunty' arrangement, Mrs Arnold thought that Joe's mother welcomed the idea since it relieved her of the pressure of regular visiting.

Mrs Arnold said her main role was to do the things that make children happy, but which the nurses had not got the time to do. She wheeled Joe round the hospital grounds, she took him to the hospital sports ground to watch cricket and football, she read to him, she took him to the Friends' canteen. But, above all, she talked to him; she talked as she fed him, as she washed him, as she undressed him, as she changed his nappies and put him to bed. She told him about her home, her shopping, the family, her dog, and everything that happened until he was as familiar with her home as were her own grandchildren. Although his speech is non-existent, Joe can make communicative noises, laughs, grunts; he can also make his interests known through facial expression. There appeared to be a real bond between Joe and Mrs Arnold, and although she did so much for him he was in no way her 'plaything', for she treated him in an adult unsentimental manner without any air of patronage.

We discussed the problems that arise when handicapped children live in a hospital ward where everything becomes communal and has to be guarded if it is to be retained, and how hospital children can become selfish unless they have some help with sharing and being kind. Mrs Arnold said that, despite Joe being handicapped and in no physical condition to ever take another child's toys or guard his own, she always took pains to explain to him about sharing and kindness to others. In order to help him to think of others she recently bought a gift for a leaving nurse, and took it to Joe's ward; she wrapped it up with him watching and then held his hand to write a card for the nurse, thanking her for her help and wishing her luck. Mrs Arnold felt that part of her role as an 'aunty' was to help Joe to be aware of the morals of living in a community; she knew he could never contribute actively to the community, but at least he would not be completely selfish.

Mrs Arnold rarely took Joe back to her own home, as he was too heavy for her to lift, and her house was a long walk from the hospital. If she bought him a present it was always clothes, books or a game which they could play together, with Joe making noises to show his choice of move. She never bought him baby toys just because he was totally handicapped. On his fifteenth birthday she had a cake made in a local baker's shop, in the shape of a boat and 'HMS Joe' written on it.

Joe's ward had many chronically handicapped brain-damaged children in it. Some of these children were described by the nurses as 'vegetables'; they were permanently in bed and quite helpless. Mrs Arnold said that she had never really thought much about the hospital environment and whether it could be better, or wondered if Joe would be better placed in a Residential Special School for cerebral palsied children. She said that the nurses were so busy that they did not have much time to talk to the children, but they were very kind and the children all seemed happy enough. She said that she had rather liked it, however, when Joe 'picked up a germ' and had had to go into isolation for several weeks. She had visited him every day there and he had been in a cubicle of his own.

Mrs Arnold thought that another drawback of ward life was that clothes she bought for Joe were sometimes put on other children, and his books got lost or torn up. To prevent this, she had recently begun bringing his personal things back to her own house when he was not using them. She did not blame the nurses for articles getting lost, she just put it down to the nurses being 'so busy that you can understand them not having time to look after personal property'.

Mrs Arnold said that her friends often wondered how she could visit such a handicapped child as Joe, but she saw nothing repulsive about him, his mind was alert and she saw him only as a person in his own right and somebody to respect; she had always received much pleasure herself from her visits and would not have continued if she had not been happy. She thought it would be nice if there were more 'aunties' for people like Joe, but it would be useless if they just started visiting as a novelty and then gave it up, for that sort of inconsistency was worse for the child than if they had never started at all.

During the five years that Mrs Arnold had been going to see Joe she had prevented him from vegetating. A nurse would not have been able to give one child that sustained individual attention over such a long period of time. Many nurses had come and gone during Joe's eight years on the ward, only the ward sister remained. Mrs Arnold brought a knowledge of the outside world to Joe, she did not wear uniform, and she had time to listen to his grunts and watch his facial expressions. She had actually helped him to communicate because she had time to listen to him. She had increased his understanding of language by reading to him for hours, and he knew many stories off by heart (she could tell he knew them because he responded with laughter or expressions of seriousness in the appropriate places). He now possessed a fund of stories and ideas in his mind which would give him thoughts throughout the long years he would inevitably have to spend in institutions. The nurses could not have done this for him.

Part Four
Questions and Answers

Introduction

Drawing conclusions from Parts Two and Three, we can see that any residential establishment which cares for severely handicapped children cannot avoid being 'institutional' in some aspects of its organization, because the children live in a crowd, they usually eat separately from the adults, and the house-parents have duty-hours, which makes them unlike real mothers and fathers. However, even if severely handicapped, the children *can* be given an existence like people outside institutions, by having: ample play opportunities; consistent mother-substitutes; an environment similar to a family home (with furniture, curtains, carpets, attractive décor and different rooms for different needs); reasonable daily routines, such as getting-up and going-to-bed times; privacy when bathing or going to the lavatory; pleasant meal-times; opportunities for being alone and achieving independence.

Residential Schools and Homes are usually organized with an emphasis on these child-care amenities, but hospitals are not, for their emphasis is traditionally on treating the sick, so long-stay children who are not ill or needing treatment will be subject to a regime which caters primarily for the unwell. The results of this regime are poor child-care standards, and we have seen from the hospital diaries how this affects the children. Analysis of child-care deficiencies in hospitals shows that they are due to a combination of:

1. *The poor-quality environment.*
2. *The duty-orientated daily timetables.* The children in Fieldway School spent two hours each day in functional routines such as going to the lavatory and bathing, but the children in Ridge Hospital spent at least six hours. And the school beds were made in the morning, then forgotten about until night-time, but the

hospital beds received lavish care all day, being straightened, tidied, re-arranged, pulled about, turned: in fact a good proportion of the nurses' working lives was devoted to cherishing beds.

3. *The changes of staff and fragmentation of care.* As well as the nurses changing wards every three months, they were also changed about every day within the ward by the sister dividing children and nurses and duties to 'give the nurses experience and make it more interesting for them'. This practice was so well-accepted that when a nurse was asked if she would like to keep to one group of children, she replied: 'Good heavens, no, how boring that would be, specially if you got the same old bunch of kids that maybe you didn't like very much anyway.'

4. *Hospital hierarchy.* The administration of hospital wards rests ultimately with people who are not in contact with the children. This was not the case at the Residential Schools, where the staff who had daily contact with the children always shared in decisions concerning their welfare. Taking responsibility from the people who actually work with the children encourages an attitude of non-involvement, so poor child-care practices will be perpetuated from one generation of staff to another. Although the Ridge Hospital nurses agreed that the out-dated practice of numbering personal effects was bad, they did not challenge the administrative staff about it; nor did they question the primitive environment, the over-crowding and degrading lavatory accommodation. There was the general feeling that 'they' would make decisions. The hierarchy did not lend itself to questions from junior staff.

The Problem

Even a brief look at the development of hospitals over the last two centuries shows that they have evolved slowly from a medley of charities, private enterprise, Poor Laws, central Government legislation and local government free choice. Hospitals are still evolving, and still trailing along with them, like a great tatty net, are the remnants of past decisions and past errors; that net catches and flings together a hotch-potch of individuals whose bodily and social misfortunes have made them helplessly dependent upon others; disabled and needy adults and children flounder on the barer reaches of the Welfare State. Unable to care for themselves they depend on us to provide, but what modern social considerations do we give them? Smug in our sophistication and education, our knowledge of child psychology, our worship of the family, our expectations of personal freedom and material comfort, snug in our Welfare State, in this bright age of legislated love unto others, have we really advanced very much in the last hundred years when we tolerate the existence of forgotten children – hidden children – only a few of whom have been described in this study?

It is the *variations in care* that are so shameful. One handicapped person can live under circumstances which give him self-respect and the respect of others, while another can live in conditions as backward as the Poor Law Workhouses and twice as shameful, for today we should know better. There are differences in care between hospitals, even between different wards in the *same* hospital; there are variations in the demands governing a child's acceptance into different schools; some Local Authorities make scant provision for their handicapped people, whilst others show particular concern and build Special Schools, Hostels, training centres and clubs. A matter of two or three miles, or even two or three roads, can make a difference to what happens to a handicapped person if the Local Authority provision is uneven. It is to be hoped that the new Chronically Sick and Disabled Persons Act, which became law in August 1970, will erase many of the inequalities in local provision, but some Authorities have so much to catch up on that the benefits have not yet been felt.

There are also variations in the *quality of staff* in the different hospitals. Teaching hospitals and acute hospitals have more choice of staff than the old long-stay chronic hospitals, because it is professionally more interesting to nurse acutely ill people than chronically handicapped people, so the acute and teaching hospitals tend to get the better educated and more interested women applying for nursing appointments. In one very large hospital with both acute and long-stay wards the staffing is arranged so that the 'better nurses' work on the acute wards, and it has not been unknown for women who have proved unsuitable for nursing on the acute wards to be given notice and transfer to a chronic ward to work out that notice. The staff and children of that long-stay ward then have to cope with a woman under notice for several weeks: she might be unstable, dishonest, incompetent to the point of being a danger to others. Of course, acute wards dealing with life and death issues must have efficient staff, but do the chronically disabled deserve to get the third-rate staff?

There are *variations in staff attitudes*. Some nurses see no need for improvements in child care and they cling on to the old regimes; some see child care only in terms of good food; others are self-critical and work individually to improve conditions. But old-fashioned regimes die hard. Visiting a hospital unit for maladjusted children I asked why there were no pictures on the walls of the ward and why the beds and lockers were so neat, there was no evidence that children lived there at all. A teacher in the unit replied: 'Well, you can't put things around, you know, after all this is a hospital and books and pictures do harbour dust and germs. And you must admit this is beautifully clean and bright.'

There were no surgical wounds to protect and no sick child ever entered that unit (the children all had behaviour problems) but that teacher, long employed in hospital schools and completely ensnared in the old fever hospital regimes, believed that it was right for maladjusted children to live in a completely bare environment.

In a seriously subnormal hospital school I saw marked variations in different classrooms. The rooms of the qualified assistants were bright, full of pictures and books and activities, whilst those of the unqualified assistants were dull and unstimulating. Asked about this variation the supervisor of the school said that the barer classrooms contained the most difficult children. It seemed a curious point that the untrained assistants were given the most difficult groups.

Staff communication varies enormously. Some hospitals hold regular teacher–nurse meetings, whilst others never do so. Some hospitals have a permanent cold war going on between teachers and nurses, a shameful schism which causes reverberating discords which unsettle the children. It is not unknown for arguments between nurses and teachers to take place in front of children.

There were variations in staff instructions regarding what to do with the children; for example, some nursing auxiliaries had been expressly told when first employed that their main job was to attend to the children's play needs. Others had never been told anything about the children's needs and when the children went back to the wards after school they were left lying about on the floor, or milling up and down in their wheel-chairs, with nothing to do.

Is it not time for social-policy-makers to try and smooth out all this uneven provision of care and attempt to achieve *equality for handicapped children*, whether they are in hospitals, schools, or under Local Authorities? Too much at present depends entirely on *chance*; a handicapped person's whole style of life can depend entirely on the luck of where he happens to live, or on what sort of people staff the institution where 'They' happen to send him.

The following sections discuss points about the present situation, and suggest possible improvements, relating to: the comprehensive role of hospital staff; Local Authority involvement; Special School responsibilities; preventing 'ghettos', and using volunteers.

The Comprehensive Role of Hospital Staff

Can the two roles of nurses and teachers in long-stay hospitals be clearly defined? In any work with children the edges between one job and another get blurred, and the different professions have to be ready to step from their traditional roles and merge with other staff. Are the deficiencies that exist in children's long-stay hospitals due to the fact that the various staff will not permit this merging, and each cling to traditional concepts?

The professions of teaching and nursing are two of the most hidebound in relation to rigid ideas and 'loyalty' to their professional roles. Perhaps this is due to the historical struggles that the two professions had in becoming established and respectable; whatever the reasons, any rigidity of ideas will affect the long-stay children.

Local Education Authority teachers in hospital schools come

under Special Education and receive a Special School increment of £137 per year, above the Burnham salary for qualified teachers. But is it good policy that any two- or three-year trained teachers can go straight from ordinary schools into hospital teaching without any additional qualification in the teaching of handicapped children, and without even having to attend a preliminary lecture or short course on the needs of handicapped children? Should all teachers in hospital schools be compelled to have extra qualifications obtained before their appointment, or agree to take further training after their first year's work in the hospital?

The answers to the questions put to teachers show that they lack interest in extra qualifications or in taking a more active part in the child's life in hospital. How can they be encouraged to take more responsibility for home-making and child care in hospitals? Accepting that some teachers have family commitments and cannot get involved in any form of residential work or after-school activities, perhaps two or three members of the hospital school staff who *are* able to do so could be given Special Responsibility Allowances or Head of Department Allowances as an encouragement to take particular interest in child care; these teachers could have special training in residential child care (under the training schemes recommended by the Williams Committee on the Staffing of Residential Homes, 1967 which would enable them to advise on child care.

At present the hospital teacher may do as little, or as much, as she likes. She can merely carbon-copy ordinary school methods into the hospital setting (perhaps suitable for the short-stay children, but not for the long-stay ones) or she can take an active part in showing the children what goes on outside the hospital.

For the long-stay child, the traditional classroom teaching technique is a sterile method of education. It may be suitable for children living at home and going to day schools (at least it is the accepted form of education in this country) but surely the long-stay hospital child should be spending the greater part of the school day away from the hospital classroom? One argument that hospital teachers use for maintaining conventional versions of school teaching is that the children will eventually return to ordinary schools so they should have as much experience of school methods as possible. But, for many children, a hospital will always be their home so they have no need to be prepared for ordinary school life.

Surely it would be better to provide something that would be of real value to them as *permanently* handicapped people, for example, lots of outings while they are still small and light enough to be comfortably taken out and carried upstairs on buses, or up a staircase in a house, or on to an escalator, and not get all tangled up with the doors of lavatories, lifts and swing-doors. If they have some real experiences of their own, they will have something to remember, something to talk about (and think about if they are speechless), when they reach that unavoidably narrow world of the permanently handicapped adult. Then the things they read about, or see on the television, or hear staff talking about, will have some relevance to them. How much more real a travel book becomes for us when we have visited the country it describes.

Another argument which teachers use to support their formal methods is that handicapped children *like* formal school and think they are doing the same things as their brothers and sisters in normal schools. But how normal is it for a child to know all about formal school work but never go on a bus or in a restaurant? The child who never experiences these things is going to be even more out of contact with his brothers and sisters, for children need more to talk about than their school-teaching routines.

If the children are in any way physically capable of leaving the hospital for a few hours each day, and many of them are, then the teachers should take them out. There should be more hospital school transport available. But surprisingly few hospital schools have their own transport especially for the children. In some instances the Variety Club of Great Britain have provided children's hospitals with 'Sunshine Coaches', explicitly for children's outings, but the coaches have not always been used for the children. Instead, they have been worn out in transporting staff, hospital equipment and even laundry. One children's hospital even gave priority use of their 'Sunshine Coach' to staff convenience, and consequently the children rarely had a chance to go out in it; a typical use made of it was to meet perfectly able-bodied staff from the railway station, a fairly short distance to walk.

One children's hospital had been in existence for more than fifty years before its school obtained its own mini-bus. Even this purchase was opposed by administrative staff on the grounds that going out was not an important part of school life. It was finally bought after many arguments, and by the voluntary efforts of a local boys' school which collected money to help pay for it.

It is a sobering thought that there are actually children in this country in 1970 who have never been into a café, never bought themselves an ice-cream, have never seen uncooked vegetables, fish and meat, or a loaf of bread. Children do not need elaborate expensive mass outings to unusual places. They can enjoy and learn merely from the daily experiences that are outside the ken of most long-stay children, unless the present old-fashioned concept of teaching in hospital is changed. Is it not time for hospital teachers to look up from their books and pictures and school equipment, and stop talking, and take their handicapped children out to see real things for themselves?

Should hospital teaching be a far wider section of education, with teachers taking responsibility in the actual administration of the hospital regarding the child-care needs of handicapped children?

With regard to parent–teacher contact, should hospital teachers who work with long-stay children have special responsibilities related to maintenance of family–child contact? For example, the teachers could make home visits, see to regular letter-writing, make telephone calls, and do all they could to keep personal contact going between the child and his family, in an effort to prevent the rejection that can result from long separation.

Letter-writing from the child to his home sometimes never gets done, because the Medical Social Worker of the hospital is not responsible for seeing that a child writes home, the nurses will leave it for the teacher to do, and the teachers may only look on letter-writing as an exercise in English and not as a means of helping to maintain family relationships. A child of four or five might spend a year in hospital without once being helped to write a note to his mother and father, because officially it is nobody's job to see it is done; even the most shaking spastic hand can be held and helped to make a kiss-sign, and parents appreciate the most humble of scribbled letters.

It is disquieting to realize that a teacher will accept lack of parental interest so phlegmatically and with no feeling that she herself might do something to foster their interest. It appears that traditional school routines – reports, timetables, stock lists – will meet with approval from hospital teachers, but anything outside purely school affairs, such as parent contact, can arouse little interest.

When Miss Y., the new Head teacher referred to on pp. 162–5 began to make contact with parents she had a small but growing response; although the hospital school had existed more than thirty years, many of Miss Y.'s parents had no idea that the hospital had a school because there had not previously been any parent–teacher contact.

There is a need for organizing Parent–Teacher Associations in all children's hospital schools. If parents live a long distance away then they should at least receive regular communications from the hospital school staff, and the family situation should be familiar to the Heads of the hospital schools. The Head of one hospital school openly admitted that he was not aware that one particular child rarely went home because he was rejected by his family and that his father had been in prison and mother had two other children to cope with; the child had been in the hospital for three years.

I know of at least four children who spent more than ten years in hospital and others who spent more than five years in hospital, but none of their parents received personal communications from the Heads of the school during those years. The pity is that small children can lose contact with their parents solely because it is nobody's particular job to try and keep contact for them. I have seen a child of five, who had daily cried inconsolably for her mother over a period of two years, upset at being put into her mother's arms; that child's contact with her mother had been so slight that when finally meeting her she did not recognize her: as she tried to get out of the arms of this 'stranger' she called, 'Mummy, mummy, I want my mummy' at the same time.

Children may go for years without receiving a letter of their own from home. Some parents think that a letter needs to be literate, and they may be reluctant to send one which they know will be read by hospital staff. Then years pass by and the child–parent relationship dwindles and is barely renewed, whereas an occasional letter to and from home and hospital might have made all the difference. Many young adults in chronic hospitals and geriatric wards may have been prevented from their final abandonment to such places, had parent–child contact been maintained in earlier years. Parents may just need helpful suggestions from the staff about the *simple* things they could do that cost very little money and involve no elaborate letter-writing, e.g. sending a weekly postcard to the child, or a piece of rock or a shell in a box when they go on holiday, or a piece of ribbon and a few big buttons in a chocolate box, even a coloured clothes' peg or last year's calendar is prized by a small child if it comes through the post from his parents. But many parents send nothing at all, because they can think only in terms of complicated letters and expensive toys which they cannot manage.

*

Where do the nursing staff fit into the problem of child care for long-stay children who do not require nursing? And why call women who look after chronically handicapped children 'nurses'? Many are not nurses at all and would far rather be called by their own names. Sometimes the mere fact of being called 'nurse' puts a label on an unqualified woman and endows her with the hospital nurse image; she then assumes an authoritarian attitude towards the children.

A Medical Social Worker in one hospital abruptly stated: 'Nurses need to be taught about children's play.' Obviously there is a need for nurses to understand about children's play and child-care, but who is going to give them this instruction? Should it be the responsibility of the teachers, with the nurses working with them during part of the day? Or should it be the responsibility of somebody specially employed by the hospital or by the Local Authority? Or should nurses attend courses of lectures at their nearest College of Education, and the Education lecturers go into hospitals and take part in nurses' training? Or should nurses working with long-stay children attend Home Office courses in residential care? The Williams Committee on the staffing of Residential Homes (1967) recommended training for all staff working in residential Homes – old people's Homes, children's Homes – but hospitals still continue to employ staff in their long-stay departments who are untrained in residential work. There are various short courses connected with training people to work with handicapped children in residential Homes (for example the Spastics Society has a staff-training college in Berkshire, which organizes regular courses for houseparents) but hospital nurses do not always have the opportunity to attend such courses: in one hospital for long-stay physically handicapped children only one nurse from the cerebral palsy department has ever been sent to attend such a course at Berkshire. If nurses do not attend courses, should the Local Authority Children's Officer go regularly into the hospital and give them lectures on child care?

How skilfully could tutor nurses and Local Authority and College of Education staff co-ordinate joint training schemes to provide for the needs of long-stay chronically handicapped children in hospitals?

On the other hand, there is a case for leaving nurses out of child care altogether and letting them concentrate on nursing only the acutely sick, and make the care of long-stay children the entire responsibility of qualified houseparents appointed by the Local Authority Children's Department, with a senior supervising houseparent resident in the hospital.

The fact that chronically handicapped children do not need nursing and should not be in hospital at all is obvious when the various costs of in-patient care are looked at. For example, in 1967–8 the weekly cost of in-patient care in subnormality hospitals was £12 5s 7d., in chronic and long-stay hospitals it was between £19 and £21 approximately, and in acute hospitals it was £45 11s 1d. And in the London Teaching Hospitals the cost of in-patient care for one week was £67 2s 10d. These figures do not prove that the long-stay chronically handicapped patients are neglected or receive third-rate treatment but rather that they do not need to be in the hospital in the first place and are not making use of the amenities of hospital care, such as surgery, pathology laboratory facilities, blood transfusions, X-rays, pharmacy and medical machinery. All that most of the long-stay patients require is day-to-day care and home accommodation.

When qualified houseparents are employed in long-stay hospitals it will ensure that the children will have trained and constant staff caring for them, instead of the untrained medley they now get: the housewives needing extra cash, the students, the pre-training employees, the language learners, the drifters. Simon Yudkin in his book *0–5: A Report on the Care of Pre-School Children* referred to middle-class families who employed '*au pair*' girls; he believed that a succession of strange girls, who often spoke little English, could be a traumatic experience for small children. How much worse it must be for handicapped children in hospital to have a constant stream of strangers caring for them during their entire childhood.

Local Authority Involvement

Handicapped children may be hospital in-patients unnecessarily, for months or even years, just because of inadequate Local Authority provision in housing, special education, and domiciliary care. Recently, a mother living in upstairs furnished rooms with two children tearfully explained how the owners of the property, living downstairs, had threatened to give her notice if her children kept thumping around above them, but with one of the children cerebral palsied and wearing calipers it was impossible to stop the noise. The hospital which the boy attended as an out-patient for physiotherapy offered to admit him as an in-patient until more suitable accommodation was found, but the mother said that she did not want him to go into hospital until absolutely necessary. Being a non-British newcomer to the area she was low on the housing list and had small hope of getting Local Authority accommodation. The hospital Medical Social Worker advised her to contact a Voluntary Society Housing Trust to see if they could help her, as the Local Authority could not offer any solution.

Mentally handicapped children may live permanently in hospitals because of inadequate provision of Local Authority training centres. When a mother has an active mentally disabled child and there is no training centre she may find it impossible to cope, especially if she has other children who have to be taken to and from school each day. Hospital in-patient care may be the only answer. If the mother is fortunate there might be a nearby psychiatric hospital with a training centre in its grounds which the child could attend as a day-child, but if not, then the child may remain an in-patient for years. The cost to the National Health Service of keeping numbers of handicapped children in hospital is an unnecessary drain on hospital resources caused by Local Authorities evading their responsibilities. Alfred Morris's Chronically Sick and Disabled Person's Act (August 1970), which makes it mandatory for Local Authorities to provide amenities at home and in the community, may correct some of the inadequacies of the past. So far, the highly valued freedom given to Local Authorities has been a typical feature of local government social services history; it means that they are free to give inadequate care, free to hand their responsibilities to the very willing hospitals, free to make their own choice of priority in expenditure, i.e. adult evening classes in car maintenance versus Special Schools for the handicapped.

Hospitals can actually hide the deficiencies of the Local Authorities by accepting responsibility for handicapped people who should be cared for in the community; in-patient care as a 'social aid' is too easily available. In 1967 the figure for children waiting to receive some kind of Special Education was approximately 14,000. Some Local Authorities have so few facilities for Special Education that their children have been known to go over 200 miles to a hospital in order to be educated.

If the Local Authority does not provide enough Special Schools then they should provide more transport to take handicapped children *daily* into nearby hospitals that have schools or training centres. One mother, with a very active, intelligent physically handicapped child was given this aid by her Local Authority: the child was picked up each morning by the Local Education Authority transport and taken to a nursery class for physically handicapped children which was being held in a local children's hospital. However, after a month or two, the Local Authority said that there were difficulties in arranging this transport and they grudgingly consented to continue it only after special pleas from the nursery-class teacher and the physiotherapists and doctors in the hospital. The mother was described by officials in the Local Education Department, and by the Head of the hospital school, as being 'like most mothers on that estate, wanting to be spoon-fed and hand her child over to the Welfare State'. This was quite untrue since that particular mother was trying hard to prevent her child becoming a permanent in-patient; she had bad health and suffered from lack of sleep caused by the disturbed sleep-pattern of the handicapped child, but she would not consent to his going into hospital care unless things got really desperate at home. The Local Authority did not appear to have taken into consideration the possibility that, if the mother's health had broken down completely it might have resulted in family break-up, with the other children going into care and perhaps the mother *and* the handicapped child becoming long-term patients in different hospitals. To provide regular transport to the hospital nursery school, to relieve that mother of the difficult child for a few hours each day, would surely have been wiser policy than waiting for the inevitable catastrophe which might have meant total family disintegration, causing high costs to the social services as well as heart-break for the family.

Local Authorities could do more to help families who have a handicapped child at home if they provided more holiday homes; a baby-sitter service to enable parents to go out together, confident that their handicapped child was safely looked after; short-term Hostel-care, perhaps just for an occasional week-end, for handicapped young adults whose families need a break from the twenty-four-hour care they have to give; and a car-service to help families who have a physically handicapped child living at home and cannot go out very far because they have not got a car. A car-service would enable the family to have an occasional trip to the country or the sea. The Report of the Committee on Local Authority and Allied Personal Social Services (1968) referred to 'children in hospitals for the mentally subnormal who could be living at home if their parents were given more support, or in Hostels if there were enough places'. In 1960 there were approximately 61,000 mentally handicapped children and adults living in hospitals for the subnormal, 1,000 in Local Authority Hostels, about 25,000 in training centres and 8,500 in welfare homes; Local Authorities hope to provide some 51,000 places in training centres in 1973 and *still* 1,000 places in Hostels.

Local Authorities could also do more to help the child who is already *permanently living in a hospital in their area*, by providing transport to get the child out of the hospital on outings, and helping the family with visiting the child. At present there are Local Authorities which have large hospitals in their areas but they take very little part in caring for the children who are living permanently in those hospitals. Will the new Morris Act for the Disabled have any powers to help here? Or will hospital in-patients and their families be excluded from the benefits of an Act making laws for Local Authorities, as in the 1948 Children's Act which does not include child care for deprived children in hospitals?

Legislation should ensure that all long-stay children come under Local Authority Children's Departments, in matters related to standards of child care, in the same way as children without families do when living in foster homes or children's Homes. At present, children who live in long-stay hospitals are not defined as a group who need child-care supervision under the 1948 Children's Act, presumably because they are not considered as being 'deprived of a normal home life'.

Local Authority Children's Departments could give practical help, too, in organizing temporary holiday foster homes for those deprived or rejected children who are in Residential Special School all the term but are re-admitted to hospitals for every school holiday because there is nowhere else for them to go when their school breaks up. It may not be commonly known, but there are numbers of handicapped children from Residential Special Schools spending school holidays in hospital wards because they have not got homes, or because their families will not (or cannot) accept them, and the Local Authority makes no provision for them. These children are particularly miserable, because they watch all the end-of-term bustle in their school, and see excited friends pack up and go off with parents, whereas the only thing that happens to *them* is that they are put into an ambulance and taken to a hospital for their holiday, to sit all day in a dull ward.

One small boy of nine arrived at a hospital for his holiday so distraught, and his voice so distorted by sobs, that nobody could understand him for several hours; it finally transpired that all he had known was that he was to 'go into hospital' and he thought he was to have an operation, and also he did not know where his father lived. 'Does my dad know where I am?' he sobbed. This little boy did not have a mother and his father moved around the country in different jobs. Some Voluntary Society Residential Special Schools remain open for school holidays, working with a skeleton staff, for the express reason of looking after these deprived family-less children.

Do long-stay hospitals, by keeping ever-open doors to rejected children, encourage the inadequacies of the Local Authorities? The cost of boarding-out a child was £2 16s. 9d. per week in 1965–6, so perhaps it is financially convenient for Local Authorities to continue to turn a blind eye to the plight of these rejected children and let the hospitals do the work in caring for them.

One of the saddest scenes I ever saw concerned the admittance of twins to a subnormality hospital. They were mentally disabled dwarfs aged forty, who had always lived at home; father had died some years before but mother had managed to look after them. Suddenly the elderly mother died and the twins had nobody to look after them so were immediately admitted to the subnormality hospital, where they would presumably live permanently. They sat on tubular steel chairs in the admissions room of the hospital, holding hands, their legs dangling, tears lying untended in the lines of their brown wrinkled cheeks. Another subnormal lady, seeing their screwed-up misery as she passed the door, handed them a child's comic she had been carrying. 'Dear little things,' she said to them. One twin held up the comic obediently and looked at it. With hurt bewildered eyes watching over the top of the comic they waited to be taken to the ward. The wards in that hospital accommodated between forty and sixty women in each, and there was very little room between the beds, even for a locker; at home the twins had lived in a cottage with small familiar furniture around them, and only mother to 'do' for them. What a contrast the big hospital would be for them. How much better it would have been had their Local Authority provided a Hostel where they could have gone. If there had been a Hostel they might have visited it and got to know the staff before their mother died, so that when they were finally alone they would have gone somewhere familiar.

Local Authorities have always valued and guarded their administrative freedom in social policy, but at what price of human misery is that freedom bought if it allows inadequacies to affect vulnerable minority groups who cannot speak for themselves?

Special School Responsibilities

The freedom to choose is also a privilege of the Residential Special Schools, this time the choice being which children they will accept. This right can be respected, since the Voluntary Society and Independent Schools are set up for specific purposes. But so long as there is a shortage of Local Authority Special Schools it is inevitable that some Special School Head teachers will 'cream off' the best of the children applying for places in their Schools. Sometimes children are turned down after very brief interviews, which leaves rejected children with no alternative but to remain in the long-stay hospitals.

One may argue that these Special Schools are within their rights to pick and choose their pupils, for if the Local Authorities do not provide Schools then it is not the job of Voluntary Societies to cover up for Local Government deficiencies by accepting all and sundry (as the long-stay hospitals do). In fact, this situation of shortage of Special Schools has earned the hospitals the reputation of 'dumping-grounds' and 'taking the dregs', because they will not refuse anybody.

The acceptable 'best' children will tend to be those from better homes, with a higher intelligence, with the more physically manageable handicap: those children who are not incontinent, who can feed themselves, and those who do not have behaviour problems. The following situation occurred recently in south-east

England: Julian, a seven-year-old boy, already having spent nearly three years in hospital, was turned down by an Independent Special School on behaviour grounds (he was over-active) with the excuse from the School that they did not consider that they would be able to manage him as he would need so much attention. They promised to 'review his situation' in one year's time; this meant another year in hospital for Julian. It is a moot point whether his maladjusted behaviour, caused initially by family discord and hospitalization, would be improved by another year in hospital – it was more than likely that yet another behaviour problem would be added to the existing difficulties. He was intelligent, able to walk and talk and his handicap of athetoid cerebral palsy did not require long-term hospital treatment, but he was living in a ward with heavily handicapped and speechless adolescents. The power that Special School Heads possess over the lives of handicapped children is disturbing when one realizes that they may be in charge of the only Special School available and that, if they refuse a child like Julian, he will stay in hospital for several years longer.

It is not unknown for some Head teachers to take children 'on trial' and then, after a term, reject them as unsuitable on grounds of behaviour, intelligence or physical management. One particular Voluntary Society Residential Special School was situated just a few miles away from a long-stay hospital and the complete contrast between the two places was astounding – the hospital was one of the old Metropolitan Asylums Board fever hospitals, short-staffed and with the usual substandard environment, whilst the school was a well-staffed, well-built showplace for that particular Society's pioneer work in educating children of a certain handicap. This School Headmaster had been known to take children from the old hospital and give them a trial in the School and then reject them and return them to the hospital (where they would spend the remainder of their childhood).

To a certain extent one may sympathize with Head teachers for wanting the more promising children, since the Schools have to 'prove themselves' to their patrons, and if they were filled with 'rejects', they would not be a good advertisement for their achievements. But the situation does conflict with the compassionate philosophies on which these Schools were founded. The business of selection, or 'creaming off' the best, is sometimes done as stringently in Special Schools as in any grammar school for ordinary children. One mother commented bitterly: 'It is as hard to get into — Special School as it might be to get into Eton or Harrow.'

The present situation in Special Education is similar to the type of divisions that bedevilled hospitals before the National Health Service, when two grades of care were available for two types of patients – the 'best' and most interesting being accepted in the acute, teaching and voluntary hospitals, whilst the chronically handicapped and socially unacceptable went to the old Workhouse infirmaries. *This system is now happening in Special Education because of the selection procedures taking place in Special Schools; it makes a hard core of rejected children accumulate en masse, in substandard conditions, in long-stay hospitals – in other words, it creates 'ghettos' in hospitals.*

Preventing 'Ghettos'

Will the problem of a hard core of rejected children remaining in hospitals ever be solved? It is possible that, even if the plans for the comprehensive District General Hospitals are developed, there will still be older institutions retaining the unwanted people who do not fit into the new plans, for there is the risk that the newly organized hospitals will not provide for the chronically handicapped homeless (young and old); these people will stay in the old institutions, again getting the poorer quality staff and buildings, again receiving third-rate semi-hospital type of care instead of Local Authority Hostel and School care. There seems to be no end to the problems of élite groups being created as opposed to the sub-groups who do not fit comfortably into either National Health hospital service or into Local Authority social services. However, could not more practical use be made of immediately available resources? For example, by mixing the *different* handicaps in the Special Schools, and even by accepting very handicapped children into ordinary day-schools?

People often raise their hands in horror if it is suggested that a grossly handicapped young person may be put in with normal children. But one adult who, in the 1930s, had been in a Special

School for convalescent tuberculosis and asthmatic children which also accepted one or two severely handicapped children recalled: 'We never really noticed Mary's handicaps, I suppose looking back on her she must have been a mentally handicapped spastic, but at the time we never thought about it, we just loved her, we used to quarrel about whose turn it was to push her wheel-chair around the playground, and at sewing time we sat round her in a circle ... she had a lovely smile but she didn't say anything or hold anything.' That very handicapped girl had obviously fitted into the school for delicate children and the adult could recall no reactions of horror from herself or the other delicate children.

There was also Zena, a heavily handicapped, very mentally backward cerebral palsied child of ten. She was on a waiting list for admission to an all-age long-stay subnormality hospital, but was admitted temporarily to a hospital unit for cerebral palsied children of average, or only a bit below average, intelligence. Zena stayed on at the unit indefinitely and attended the hospital school with the other cerebral palsied children, although by Ministry of Education rulings she was considered 'unsuitable for education'. Zena was quite unable to do anything for herself; at six she was functioning like a six-month-old baby, throwing toys off her table, squeezing soft toys and balls, sometimes squealing with delight and sometimes shaking with silent giggles. At the age of ten she showed only slight improvement. Her face was brown and pleasant, framed by a mass of black shining curls which set off her attractive eyes. She spent more than five years in that hospital unit and was always accepted as part of the school group; she watched the classroom activities and always appreciated what went on. She got excited about Christmas decorations, Easter parties, cookery time and picnics, and once, when a nature exhibition took place in the hospital and Zena identified every tree in the grounds as being a 'mima' (the only word she said) such was the affectionate acceptance of Zena that the other children insisted on solemnly labelling an unknown twig as a piece of 'mima tree' and entered it in the show.

To have excluded Zena would have been totally unjust; she obtained a lot of stimulation from mixing with the mentally able children, and she received affection and attention from everybody. That attention made her a person, as opposed to a dull 'patient', which is what she would have been had she gone to a big understaffed subnormality ward with fifty other children of the same poor abilities and physical handicaps as her own. The child Lu-Lu could have benefited from the chance that Zena had been given. And the arrangement did not cost the National Health Service any more than it would have done had Zena been sent to the subnormality hospital straight away.

Mixing the differently handicapped children could be done more everywhere if only teachers and administrative staff and Heads of Homes and Schools would permit it. Just one or two severely handicapped people going into other groups would help to prevent the ghettos of people crowded together with all the same chronic handicaps. Many teachers and nurses working with boys who have muscular dystrophy disagree with special units for these boys, because the handicap is progressive and eventually the young people realize their time is limited as they see their contemporaries weaken. Some teachers in muscular dystrophy units report boys in their late teens arguing about who should have the belongings of a boy who was rapidly weakening.

Infant-age hospitalized children with mental and/or physical handicaps could be helped if they were accepted for daily school in ordinary little infant schools, which had easily negotiable classrooms on the ground floor, and staff who would be willing to accept one or two children who were living permanently in hospitals. The children could be transported daily from the hospital, and would have the opportunity to experience the play and speech and friendship of ordinary children with wide interests and family homes. Such a scheme would probably meet with opposition from some teachers and parents, but with courage it could be done effectively and its benefits to the handicapped children would be immeasurable; also, the community would become accustomed to the nature of handicaps.

If infant-school teachers were paid Special School allowances for co-operating in such a hospital-children/day-school scheme, it might be an added incentive towards making the scheme a success. Will the Education (Handicapped Children) Act, which came into operation in April 1971, do anything to help in integrating the handicapped with the able, or will it merely continue to perpetuate the many-sided system of Special Education which is in operation at present?

*

It is usual for the ward organization of the big all-age mental subnormality hospitals to segregate the patients into groups according to age and sex. Occasionally, a newspaper journalist will jump on a story of a child being 'locked up in a ward with adult mental patients'. An outcry is raised and the child is promptly put back into the children's ward. But is it so shocking for children to be mixed with adults? Is it not really the most natural thing in the world for groups of humans to be mixed in ages? Did we not mix with adults when we were children – our uncles, aunts, grandmothers and grandfathers? Did our parents not sometimes leave grandmother to put us to bed, bath us, teach us to feed and dress ourselves? Did we not all, at some time, walk down the shops with a grandfather or an uncle? Do not most families behave like this still? How offended a family would be if a newspaper story was made of their ordinary family behaviour, accusing it of being bad. But if a mentally handicapped child is found in the adult wards of a subnormality hospital people can rarely look upon those handicapped adults in the hospital with him as being his substitute aunts and uncles who might teach him how to dress, to eat, look after him at bedtime, and comfort him when he falls, in the same way that our own aunts and uncles did. Are mentally handicapped children to be denied their *rights* (which are the normal rights of all human beings) to be part of a *mixed human group*, solely because of hospital regimes which segregate the ages and sexes?

By thinking that segregation of the ages and sexes is the only way to organize our big all-age subnormality hospitals we are merely adding another deprivation to the already grossly deprived child's life. Have we any right to prevent a child from experiencing the affection and attention of interested adults? A child in an ordinary family situation learns behaviour by making relationships with adults who remain constant in his world; he will become responsible because he responds to the approval and the expectations of a group of interested adults. He experiences adult reactions to his behaviour, their anger, loving, praising, grumbling, and he learns to adapt his own behaviour to their reactions. But this normal adult–child learning situation is denied the mentally handicapped child when he lives entirely in a children's ward. 'But he has the nurses,' people say. But can nurses always do this teaching? Remember the shortages of staff; remember, too, the hospital organization that moves nurses from ward to ward; nurses work in shifts; there are part-time nurses; holidays have to be taken; nurses give notice and leave; remember these things, consider the ever-changing staff in chronic hospitals and ask who are the most constant people in the hospital. The answer is, the adult patients, many of whom live in the hospital for twenty years or more.

So, surely it would be more helpful than harmful if some of the mentally handicapped children lived in wards with the adults, who would be able to provide the child with individual attention in the same way as any child gets attention from his aunts and uncles?

Dr John Gibson, of St Lawrence's Hospital, in Caterham, Surrey, is an outspoken critic of the present custom of segregating ages in hospitals, but he has met with some opposition. His words: 'The worst place to put a mentally-retarded child may be in a ward with other mentally-retarded children' are contained in an essentially compassionate paper which Dr Gibson wrote for *Clinical Pediatrics*. But these words are explosive to some hospital administrators who continue to believe in strict segregation of adults from children. Elsewhere in his paper Dr Gibson wrote: 'One of the commonest criticisms of any hospital for the mentally retarded is that it segregates patients from the community, from the world outside, from ordinary life. Furthermore, what nearly always happens inside is another kind of segregation: man from woman, adolescent from middle-aged, middle-aged from old, child from adult, little girl from little boy. Is all this necessary? Would any harm come, would any good come, if they were mixed up more?' and: 'It is possible that this mixing might be good for every child. There may be children who do not fit into family units, as there are some old people who might not like to be with the young. But the experiment can be tried.'

The handicapped adults also benefit from the chance of having a child to care for; it gives them an extra sense of purpose and an interest in life. Dr Gibson has found that when a child is put into an adult ward there is always one particular adult who 'adopts' the child, whilst the other adults help her; supervised by the nurses, this 'ward-aunt' looks after 'her' child's feeding, dressing, washing and general care and training. The arrangement mutually benefits the adult and the child, and releases the nurse from some of her responsibilities. Before the arrangement takes place, the parents of the child are always asked for permission. Dr Gibson believes this scheme could be profitably extended to mixing mentally handicapped children into old people's Homes, for it might well be better for a small mongol child to go and live in an old people's Home rather than in the children's ward of a large subnormality hospital. But no doubt such an idea would cause an outcry of protest.

Some may argue that Dr Gibson's theories merely disguise the many flaws and deficiencies in the present hospital system and Local Authority provision, such as the short and unqualified staff, poor buildings, and lack of hostel accommodation. Some may argue that it is a step back to the old Poor Law Workhouses days, when adults and children were mixed together in the infirmaries. Others may argue that it is a form of cheap labour to make up for shortages of staff, i.e. using adult patients as child-minders. Some say it could be dangerous for the children because adult patients might assault them; but the chances of this happening are no higher than in the world outside the hospital, and obviously a child would not be put into wards where patients are known to be dangerous. To conclude that all mentally handicapped adults are potentially dangerous shows total lack of understanding.

Is it kind that mentally handicapped adults should always be denied the experience of caring for a child of their 'own', merely because they have been born mentally disabled? What sort of system tolerates the cruel absurdity of a ward accommodating between forty and fifty children, guarded by a nurse and an auxiliary (they can only 'guard' when faced with so many backward children in a mass), whereas in an upstairs ward sit forty women doing their little bits of weaving and knitting, their poor old lives as empty as when they first entered the hospital as children themselves thirty or forty years ago? Would it really be so bizarre if two or three of the children were taken upstairs to live in the ladies' ward, to be cared for by adults who have never before had the opportunity to care for a child?

Florence Nightingale, one of whose principles was that hospitals should never 'harm the patients', was against segregating children into children's wards and hospitals. In her essentially practical wisdom she recognized that the needs of young children, essentially bound up with experiencing the security of a family style of life, can only be met by the child having the care of attentive adults rather than living in a room with many other similarly affected children.

Because of the constantly changing staff and the work rotas in the big subnormality hospitals, a child may have one nurse get him up, another put him to bed, a third give him his lunch, yet another his tea, another may bath him, and a strange face may see to him when he cries in the night. But if he lived in a ward with adult patients he would have a group of permanent adults around him, and thus feel more secure. If the child woke in the night and needed comforting he would see the familiar face of his own 'ward-aunt' in a bed near him, and would feel more secure at the sight of her than at the sight of a night-nurse whom he may never have seen before and who might not know his name or even speak English (I have sometimes asked normally intelligent physically handicapped children the name of their night-nurse and they have not known, all they could tell me was that she was not English). If there was a 'ward-aunt' the child's toilet routine could be more normal, too; she would see the child wriggling and needing the lavatory and would take him to the big lavatory herself and wait until he had finished. This would prevent his regimentation on a plastic pot in a room with dozens of other children all sitting in rows on similar yellow plastic pots. What could be more normal than for a child to be balanced on a grown-up lavatory with an aunt waiting nearby until he finishes, in the same manner as most of us received our lavatory training?

In Caterham I saw a mentally handicapped man holding the hand of his 'own' boy as they walked together across a field; the man sat down and gently grumbled at the youngster for undoing his shirt and did it up for him again. The boy sat contentedly on the garden seat next to him, and the adult turned to another man, in a wheel-chair nearby, and talked about the child; both grown-ups were interested in the boy and were enjoying a common purpose in looking after him for the morning. Had the child been in a ward with two harassed nurses and forty to fifty other mentally handicapped children he would have sat unattended on the floor, perhaps rocking, perhaps undressing, or picking himself abusively; nobody would have had time to make sure that his clothes stayed on; nobody would have been able to leave all the other children in order to walk him across the field in the sunshine. None of the children would have talked together as companions, so he would have heard no words, only the endless battering unproductive noise typical of a room full of unoccupied seriously subnormal children would have filled his ears.

In a woman's ward at Caterham I saw a spastic child lying on a blanket, with a woman patient sitting sewing near him. Another woman was watching the boy and saw him roll over, so she attracted the attention of his 'ward-aunt' who went across and turned him back again. This group of mentally handicapped ladies had been given purpose in their lives by having that child in the ward with them – he had become like their own child.

Dr Gibson has plans for converting a building in the grounds of St Lawrence's Hospital to make it into a home for a small group of mentally handicapped men, women and children. These residents will live together in shared accommodation, their food will be cooked on the premises and everything will be made as much like a home as possible, only the bedroom accommodation will be separate. The adults will help to dress, bath, feed, and play with the children; and they will take the children to the hospital school each morning, a short walk across the grounds, and will meet them again outside school in the afternoon. They will be the most permanent people in the children's lives, as much like a real family as possible.

Although not the complete answer, it would seem that Dr Gibson's theory is a simple, compassionate and *immediate* aid to solving some of the problems of long-term institutional care caused by staff shortages and 'ghetto-formation'. While we search and plan for more elaborate and expensive ideas of solving the problems of over-crowded hospitals (there are always between 50,000 and 60,000 patients in mental subnormality hospitals) we may tend to forget that each day there are already young patients getting older and old patients dying, all living segregated affectionless lives. Until purpose-built mixed hostels are provided in the community for all the mentally handicapped people who should not, anyway, be living inside hospitals, it would surely be the most broad-minded policy to mix the ages in the hospitals themselves? After all, two of the greatest and most normal experiences of human life are for an adult to love and help a child, and for a child to love and trust an adult. What sort of sterile existence does society give the mentally handicapped when it condemns them to life-long segregation into their own age-groups?

Using Volunteers

How can voluntary workers be made more use of in helping long-stay hospital children, both the mentally and the physically handicapped? One way would be for families to become week-end 'foster-families'. Family-less long-stay children particularly need experience of a family situation and regular access to a normal home. Because of the insecurity already suffered by deprived children, the organizers would have to take care that any befriending family remained consistent in their interest in the child, and at no time should the idea be tolerated that the handicapped child was a passing novelty to be put down after a few months when the interest had worn off, for with long-stay children the contact may last for five years or longer. It would also be important that the foster-family did not complicate the child's own tenuous family relationship (if he had any). Possibly, such a scheme would need the co-ordinating advice of the Local Authority Children's Department, as well as being initially organized by the hospital's Voluntary Services Organizer.

The fostering family might not be able to have the handicapped child sleeping at home with them, but they might be able to have him with them in the daytime for a number of regular week-ends each year; to have a complete day with a family would open up a new world to children who live in hospital. I remember taking a small group of long-stay children out to tea at the house of a voluntary worker, and they were remarkably quick to appreciate the littleness and 'chintziness' of a small suburban home. One child wanted to keep going upstairs to look at the bedroom, and when she was taken up all she wanted to do was to stroke the candlewick bedspreads. Another child, aged six, was amazed at the smallness of the bathroom and wash-basin and found joy in touching the soft coloured toilet-paper; we had to lift him up again and again to show him the view from the bathroom window down the long narrow tree-cramped garden; he had never looked from an upstairs window into a suburban garden before. All the children peered into the small pantry, and felt down the sides of the patterned upholstered sofa, and stared under the low beds at the enclosed soft darkness beneath. When children live in bare, unpatterned, light hospitals, then they find a sensuous joy in the darkness and softness of an ordinary home which they have not experienced before.

If a foster-family scheme was organized it would not immediately solve all problems, but it might at least prevent the following painful situation from being repeated. Caren was a postpoliomyelitis child who had been hospitalized in an orthopaedic ward for eight years; she was nearly nine and was confined to a wheel-chair with paralysis from the waist down. Her ward was organized with the usual hospital routines, beds in two long rows, early rising, undressing soon after school finished at 3.30, and so on. One day Caren was taken to visit a farm for the day, with about ten other handicapped children from another ward. The visit had been talked about for several weeks, one of the children of the farm family was herself handicapped and the family was well used to coping with children in wheel-chairs. The day was sunny and a picnic tea was laid on the lawn outside the kitchen door. The other children, who had been to the farm several times before, started their picnic with the farm family sitting down with them and helping. But Caren, quite unused to being out of the hospital ward, fearful of animals, and unaccustomed to strange farm smells and the muddle of a picnic, was in an environment which seemed as strange and dangerous to her as a trip to the moon. She reacted by setting up a distressed non-stop high-pitched whine of 'Take me back to the ward, I'm not supposed to be here, what am I doing here, I should be in my ward, take me back to the ward.' It was not possible to transport her back immediately, so for the rest of the afternoon she wailed, lost and miserable in her unfamiliar surroundings. After eight years in a hospital ward Caren was totally unable to enjoy an ordinary family picnic in a farm garden. Her peculiar distressful reaction appeared even more grotesque occurring as it did against the background of such a normal happy garden scene.

A foster-family scheme could also be used for those children from Residential Special Schools who have to spend their school holidays in hospitals because they have no homes or families of their own. If they had a foster-family with whom they could spend at least part of every school holiday then they would feel that they had somewhere safe and familiar of their own, instead of just going to hospitals; their foster-family could also take an interest with writing letters and sending birthday cards to the deprived child.

There are many ways in which volunteers can be used – as hospital 'aunts', shopping helpers, drivers, ward-helpers. Already they give valuable aid in a variety of ways, but until every hospital appoints a Voluntary Services Organizer as an essential, instead of an unusual, addition to the staff, then there will be many potential volunteers never discovered, or made insufficient use of; and how many Carens will be left to find normal experiences terrifying?

A Child's Questions

Jason was five. Cerebral palsy had given him permanently writhing limbs and slurred speech. Family rejection had given him a never-eased home-sickness. Social provision gave him a hospital to live in. A lively mind gave him an insatiable curiosity about the world.

'Why can't I purr like a kitten?' he asked. This was fairly easy to answer.

'Why did my mummy eat me?'

'*Eat* you?' This was startling.

'Yes, you told me yesterday I was in her tummy when I was a baby, how did I get there, did she eat me?'

After a while this was sorted out to our mutual satisfaction.

'Where do I keep my tears when I am not using them?' This was a little harder. He may well wonder where they came from, for he had known more tears than most of us.

'Why *do* I get sad such a lot of times?' All the pat answers from past experience with inquisitive infant children could not rescue me very comfortably from this question.

'Have I got to stay all my life in this hospital?' What answer now? I thought of all the brave reforms throughout social history, the early crude attempts to help the destitute and improve Workhouses, housing and factories. There were all the Committees, Members of Parliament, journalists, civil servants, the charities, the wealthy and the poor, whose opinions and ideals had shaped English social history over the last 200 years. There were Children's Acts, Housing Acts, Education Acts, Mental Health Acts, the National Health Service, and Acts for Divorce, Criminal Justice and Abortion; there were laws to protect women, homosexuals, animals, immigrants, house purchasers, landlords, street vendors and car-drivers; the twentieth century – the age of humane reasoning and compassion. But where did young Jason and his kind fit into this good age of reform and broad thinking?

'You're not answering me. *Will* I have to stay all my life in this hospital? Answer me ...'

Bibliography

Abel-Smith, B., *The Hospitals 1800–1948* (London, 1964).

Barton, R., *Institutional Neurosis* (Bristol, 1959).

Bowlby, J., *Maternal Care and Mental Health*, World Health Organization Monograph Series No. 2, 2nd edn (Geneva, 1952).

Burlingham, D. and Freud, A., *Infants Without Families* (London, 1944).

Davis, B., *Social Needs and Resources in Local Services* (London, 1968).

Gibson, J., 'The Mentally Retarded Child in Hospital', *Clinical Pediatrics*, Vol. 8, No. 5, May 1969.

Jones, K., *Mental Health and Social Policy 1845–1959* (London, 1960).

Paige, D. and Jones, K., *Health and Welfare Services in Britain in 1975* (Cambridge, 1966).

Pinker, R., *English Hospital Statistics 1861–1938* (London, 1966).

Pritchard, D. G., *Education and the Handicapped 1760–1960* (London, 1963).

Raynes, N. V. and King, R. D., 'The Measurement of Child Management in Residential Institutions for the Retarded'. Paper given by N. Raynes at the First Congress of the International Association for the Scientific Study of Mental Deficiency, Montpellier, 1967.

Robb, B., *Sans Everything* (London, 1967).

Slack, K. M., *Social Administration and the Citizen* (London, 1969).

Tizard, J., *Community Services for the Mentally Handicapped* (Oxford, 1964).

Tizard, J., 'Residential Care for the Mentally Retarded'. Paper given at the First Congress of the International Association for the Scientific Study of Mental Deficiency, Montpellier, 1967.

Tizard, J., King, R. D., Raynes, N. V. and Yule, W., 'The Care and Treatment of Subnormal Children in Residential Institutions'. Paper given by J. Tizard at the International Conference of Association of Special Education, London, 1966.

Townsend, P., *The Last Refuge* (London, 1962).

Yudkin, S., *0–5: A Report on the Care of the Pre-school Child* (London, 1967).

Report of the Care of Children Committee (Curtis) Cmnd 6922, 1946 (HMSO).

Report of the Committee on Local Authority and Allied Personal Social Services (Seebohm) Cmnd 3703, 1968 (HMSO).

Report of the Williams Committee on the Staffing of Residential Homes (London, 1967).

Health and Welfare. The Development of Community Care, Cmnd 3022, 1966 (HMSO).

The Health of the School Child 1966–1968: Report of the Chief Medical Officer of the Department of Education and Science, 1969 (HMSO).

A Census of Patients in Psychiatric Beds: Eileen Brooke, Report on Public Health and Medical Subjects, N.116: Ministry of Health, 1963 (HMSO).

Annual Report of the Department of Health and Social Security for the year 1968: Part One: Health and Welfare Service. Cmnd 4100 (HMSO).

Report on Hospital in-Patient Enquiry for the year 1966: Part One Tables, Ministry of Health and General Register Office (HMSO).

A Report on Voluntary Work in Hospitals: Jan Rocha, Organisers of Voluntary Services in Hospitals: King's Fund Report, 1968.

Deprivation of Maternal Care: A Reassessment of its Effects: Public Health Paper No. 14. World Health Organization (Geneva, 1962) (this publication contains a comprehensive reference to research and writings on childhood deprivation published up to 1962).

More about Penguins and Pelicans

Penguinews, which appears every month, contains details of all the new books issued by Penguins as they are published. From time to time it is supplemented by *Penguins in Print*, which is a complete list of all available books published by Penguins. (There are well over four thousand of these.)

A specimen copy of *Penguinews* will be sent to you free on request. For a year's issues (including the complete lists) please send 30p if you live in the United Kingdom, or 60p if you live elsewhere. Just write to Dept EP, Penguin Books Ltd, Harmondsworth, Middlesex, enclosing a cheque or postal order, and your name will be added to the mailing list.

Note: *Penguinews* and *Penguins in Print* are not available in the U.S.A. or Canada

The Safety of the Unborn Child

Geoffrey Chamberlain

The unborn child is usually perfectly safe. However, various risks are occasionally given publicity, and these often build up to become major worries to the pregnant woman. Often she feels that it would be childish and time-wasting to air these problems to others but they remain in her mind.

This book gives a straight presentation of the hazards to the unborn child, assesses them, and displays them against the background of normality. It therefore deals with material not often discussed outside the confines of the consulting room, and sometimes not discussed frankly enough even there. It is offered as a practical contribution to the understanding of pregnancy, and also in the hope of allaying many unspoken worries of pregnant women.

Man, Medicine and Environment

René Dubos

In this book Dr Dubos, an editor of the *Journal of Experimental Medicine*, examines the environmental forces affecting the history of social groups from the precursors of *homo sapiens* to man today. Considering characteristics unique to humanity, he states that 'Man can function well only when his external environment is in tune with the needs he has inherited from his evolutionary, experiential, and social past, and with his aspirations for the future.' As man acquires much of his personality through responses to environment, Dr Dubos discusses the complex interrelations that govern life today, and the effects of environment on the health of primitive and modern man. In non-technical language he surveys the control of life, biomedical philosophies and the possibilities of a science of man. Precisely because they are concerned with various aspects of humanity, Dr Dubos believes that 'the biomedical sciences in their highest form are potentially the richest expression of science'.

Not for sale in the U.S.A. or Canada